John Parker,
Missionary Statesman

by

Charlene H. West
Edna Parker

John Parker,
Missionary Statesman

Text: The Holy Bible
New King James Version

Published by

Revelation Northwest Publishers
6909 Fawn Canyon Drive
Oklahoma City, Oklahoma 73162
USA

Printed in the United States of America

ISBN 13: 978-1497413719
ISBN 10:1497413710

Charlene H. West, B.A., M.L.S.
WestCharlene@att.net
with
Edna Parker

John Parker,
Missionary Statesman

Go therefore and make disciples of all the nations,
baptizing them
in the name of the Father
and of the Son and of the Holy Spirit,
Teaching them to observe all things
that I have commanded you; and lo,
I am with you always,
even to the end of the age.
Amen.

Matthew 28:19, 20

Table of Contents

Chapter One
A Year of Global Impact

It was 1927, a year of global impact. In that awesome year Charles Lindbergh made his solo flight across the Atlantic. Television was first demonstrated successful in New York City, and in Rocky Mount, North Carolina, a second son was born to Roy Cleveland and Lillie Haney Parker.

Lillie Haney was originally from Tallahassee, Florida, but times were difficult there. Jobs were scarce, and the pay was not sufficient to support a family. News reached Florida that factories in North Carolina were employing young women as well as men. Lillie and her older sister Carlee along with Gladys, the youngest, decided to migrate to look for jobs. Carlee and Lillie were barely old enough to work, and Gladys would have to wait until she was older. These three Christian girls took the train from Florida to Rocky Mount, North Carolina.

They put their lives in the hands of the Lord, and they knew that He would protect them as well as help them get settled in their new location. Looking

1

back Lillie and Carlee were both thoroughly con-vinced that God had helped them find jobs in a fac-tory making socks and had also helped them secure their housing in Tarboro, North Carolina. The girls soon found a church home, and they were faithful in their attendance as well as in supporting the church by giving their tithes and offerings to God. They were fully committed to giving their work a full day, so why shouldn't they also give their best to God?

Certainly it was not by accident that there was a young man named Roy Cleveland Parker who also had a job at that same factory. He soon noticed these beautiful girls from the state of Florida and was es-pecially drawn to Lillie who was four years younger than he. Since they were also attending the same church, it was easy to get acquainted and have a time of fellowship. This, however, soon developed into something warmer, and in 1923 the courtship of Roy Cleveland and Lillie ended in marriage.

Their second son was born on June 5, 1927. His name "John" came right from the Bible, but his mid-dle name was "Bertram" after Bertram C. Brown. Rev. Brown was the pastor of the small church the family attended and where Cleveland and Lillie were married. Incidentally, John's family always called him by his middle name, Bertram.

Their family grew until there were three boys and five girls. Roy's work kept him busy providing for his family, but Lillie was a spiritual power-house in the home. She read the Bible and prayed with her children while she instilled within their lives the principles of Christian discipline. For some time they lived three miles from the church, but Lillie would get her little flock together and walk with them the three miles to service on Sunday mornings. They also walked back home again after the meeting was over – a six-mile round trip. Sometimes they made the trip again on Sunday night when they had special revival services. It is interesting that Cleveland never owned an automobile!

Lillie's favorite reading material was the *Advocate*, the official magazine of the church. She devoured it every month from cover to cover and shared those things she felt would be important or of interest to her family. She did her best to keep up-to-date with what was going on in World Missions, and she loved to share with her children the real live stories from the missionaries. Little did Lillie realize the impact that her "around-the-world" teachings would have on her children – especially on John.

Lillie's health, however, was very fragile. Her youngest baby died at birth, and by that time her strength was drained to the limit. At home again she tried to take over where she had left off, but she no longer had the physical strength to carry on. At the age of 34, on John's 12th birthday, she went to meet the Lord she so dearly loved. Her life had been given to Him in loving service, and she knew that if she physically died and left her earthly home, she would be with the Lord in her heavenly home.

So we are always confident, knowing that while we are at home in the body we are absent from the Lord. For we walk by faith, not by sight. We are confident, yes, well pleased rather to be absent from the body and to be present with the Lord. Therefore we make it our aim, whether present or absent, to be well pleasing to Him.

(2 Corinthians 5:6-9).

Needless to say, Lillie's passing brought tremendous changes in the home. The children, even at that early age, realized that their father had to be on his job at the Atlantic Coast Line Railroad Repair Shop. It was summer vacation, and the children at home did their part in helping their father get their new life in order. Each one cooperated to keep things going, including the cooking, household duties, laundry, and the vegetable garden. More changes came, however, when summer vacation ended and school started. The two youngest weren't ready for school, so they had to stay with Aunt Carlee.

John (12 years old) and Wiley (14) took turns making breakfast and getting the children off to school. John had to miss school once a week to do the family laundry, and if the weather was too bad for the clothes to dry, it sometimes meant missing another day! John kept his grades up, however, and never missed passing to his next grade. During the summer while his classmates were free to travel, play or just be lazy, John worked on his Aunt Leonia's farm to earn enough money to buy his clothes for the next school year. He was able later to get a job where his father worked, and then he began to help with the household expenses. He kept this schedule through High School until he graduated at the age of 17 with high honors. He realized, however, that in the future he would be on his own financially.

In July of 1944, John made a full surrender of his life to the will of God. This happened during a revival conducted by Rev. N. J. Ward, at which time God also called him to preach. From that beginning he was, at least potentially, a preacher. Although he understood the need to prepare himself for the task of reaching others for Christ, he had no financial resources to draw from.

In the fall of 1944, he enrolled in Holmes Bible College. This institution at that time operated by faith and was available to those who wanted to prepare themselves by just giving according to their means. Perhaps it was for this reason that this institution produced some of the church's greatest leaders. John went with one purpose and ideal – that of being the best preacher and servant of God he could possibly be. He later laughed and said that far too often, he aimed his arrows at the sun and they fell in the mud! But his eyes were always on the goal.

During his first year at Holmes something crystallized in John's spirit that he had known for a long time—a concern for the lost people of other lands and cultures. He had never forgotten how his mother had shared about the men and women who had gone as missionaries to foreign countries. But where did they go, and what did they do? He found some important scriptures in the Bible where Jesus Himself gave him the answer he needed from His Word:

Go therefore, and make disciples of all the nations, baptizing them in the name of the Father and of the Son and of the Holy Spirit, teaching them to observe all things that I have commanded you; and, lo, I am with you always, even unto the end of the age (Matthew 28:19, 20).

Ye shall be witnesses unto me both in Jerusalem, and in all Judea, and in Samaria, and unto the uttermost part of the earth (Acts 1:8).

John was at Holmes as a student preparing for the ministry of the Word, so he began his work in his Jerusalem – where he was presently living. He spent his summers ministering both in established churches and in new evangelistic efforts—in his Judea and in Samaria.

John knew, however, that he was destined to preach the gospel on foreign soil, and that his work would eventually take him to other lands. God had already given him a heart for regions beyond the boundaries of his own country. He would tell those who spoke different languages and lived in other nations that Jesus loved them. The Lord seemed to be saying China, and he was willing to go even there. He would go to the place of God's choosing in His own timing. John had been born with a specific purpose, and God had designed him to serve according to His will.

So why was the birth of John Parker in the year of 1927, along with other outstanding world events, a matter of global impact? How would his life make a difference that could be considered global?

The truth of the matter is that John Parker had a message of interest for the whole world. It was that Jesus died and paid the debt for the sins of every person. Jesus rose again conquering death, hell and the grave, and He provided salvation for all who would believe. John Parker was completely dedicated to reach others with this message and to train them to share it. With that goal, He became a minister and missionary with a world-wide outreach for Christ. The life of John Parker was destined to be global!

> *There is no ocean too wide,*
> *No mountain too steep,*
> *No climate too cold or hot,*
> *No circumstance too difficult or unpleasant,*
> *Go we must, and tell we must.*

There was no other option; John Parker's mission would be global, because he would respond to God's global call. He would go!

Chapter Two
Getting Ready for the Future

During John's senior year at Holmes while attending the Falcon Camp Meeting, one of his friends introduced him to a student named Edna Harrell. She was already enrolled to begin studying at Holmes at that time, but little did she realize the impact this tall, handsome young man was to have on her life. And he wondered who this young lady was.

Edna was born in Garland, North Carolina, where she lived until she finished the seventh grade. Her father was a railroad man, so he moved around a great deal. She was saved when she was about 13 years old. While they were living in Wilmington, North Carolina, where she attended High School, she became a member of the Pentecostal Holiness Church.

After graduating from High School, Edna continued to prepare herself academically. She began attending Emmanuel College in 1940, and in 1942 she graduated from that Christian institution located in the state of Georgia, and she went on to East Carolina University where she graduated with a BA in Elementary Education. It was after teaching two years that Edna decided to attend Holmes Bible College in Greenville, South Carolina. Little did she realize that this move was surely ordered by the Lord.

She enrolled at Holmes, and since she had a teacher's certificate, the officials accepted her as a student with the understanding that she would teach two classes to undergraduates. How happy she was with this arrangement! She felt it was just what the Lord wanted. Certainly God had prepared her for this type of Christian service! Edna adjusted well to life at Holmes, and she felt that the Lord was daily guiding her steps.

During the first revival of the year, there was a great outpouring of the Holy Spirit as students prayed for direction concerning their future work. Edna also felt burdened to seek an answer concerning her own future in God's kingdom.

It was in a revival service conducted by Francis Shelby and her co-worker, that Edna received a call to Christian service. She felt God had a special work for her to do, but she wasn't convinced that she was cut out for it. She thought that there might not be a place for her since she couldn't sing or play the piano, and she gave the Lord all kinds of excuses as to why she couldn't accept a call to Christian service. At the same time, however, she was seeking the Lord in this time of revival. She would be one of the first to the altar and one of the last to leave as she struggled to be sure of God's call. One night, however, it got late, and the chaperon let her and the girls praying with her know that it was time to go to their rooms.

As they marched from the church to the dormitory, Edna and her friends continued to pray. On entering the building the matron, Miss Ruth Heath, instead of sending them to their dorm rooms surprisingly opened the door to the chapel and directed them in. She told them that they could continue to pray there and seek the Lord. What a blessing, because that night God mightily answered!

As they prayed, Edna felt the Lord was asking her to be a missionary, and each time she would say *No!* one of the girls would say *Yes!* She wanted to fully follow the Lord, but she wanted to be sure she wasn't making a mistake. She was certainly well equipped educationally, but she began telling the Lord that she didn't have any talents—that she couldn't sing or play the piano. Each time the Lord would say, What if everyone just sang and played the piano? She was having a very hard time answering the Lord.

She felt that He was winning, so she said, *Yes, Lord, I'll be a missionary; Yes, Lord, I'll go to China. But Lord, I can't go alone.* God assured her that she would not be alone. He, Himself, would work out the details. He just impressed her to give her life to Him and to be a willing and obedient servant.

After becoming willing to give herself to the Lord in Christian service and to even go as a missionary, she had her questions. How would she prepare? And what kind of preparation would she need?

It was in chapel one day that she saw John Parker come in for service, and the Lord spoke to her and said, *That man* will be your husband. Although they had met, and she had been impressed with this tall, handsome young man, she didn't think that he had been interested in her! She must have been mistaken, however, because the interest was there. A spark had been struck, but the timing was not yet right.

John had entered Holmes in 1944, but after much work and hard study, he graduated with his Bachelor's degree in Theology. He felt his next step was to apply for credentials with the North Carolina Conference.

John was granted ordination in August of 1947 and was assigned as pastor to the Bethel Pentecostal Holiness Church. It was a wonderful group of people. He was there as their preacher and teacher, but those people were also a blessing him. Some of these wonderful people turned out to be efficient teachers for him! In this first pastorate, he was putting into practice what he had learned in the classroom. John was a young pastor who had not yet reached the magic age of 21, but he was also a great student and an apt learner!

One day John found a scripture that he took to heart, and it helped him make an important decision for the work God had for him. It came as good advice from the Apostle Paul to young Timothy, his son in the Lord.

Be diligent [study] *to present yourself approved to God, a worker who does not need to be ashamed, rightly dividing the world of truth* (2 Timothy 2:15)

John felt the Lord was speaking to him. He needed to study and he felt directed to continue his education. He enrolled at East Carolina University and began working toward a B.S. degree in English, and he would continue on and get his Master's degree. His pastorate at Bethel would extend from 1947 until 1951, but meanwhile, something of vital and profound importance took place in his life.

John never forgot what his calling was. When the time was right, he would go to regions beyond the boundaries of his own nation. He knew, also, that the choosing of his life partner would be the most important decision of his life outside of accepting the Lord as His Savior and obeying God's call. He had not forgotten Edna. She had a call to China even as the Lord had called him. On one of their first dates, John had mentioned that since they were both called to China, they might just as well go together! On June 21, 1949, he and Edna Grace Harrell were married.

Edna was exactly the partner John needed, and she was just right in her role as a pastor's wife. Certainly this was a part of the training God had for them in preparation for their future work.

They were always conscious that they shared a missionary call from the Lord, and that at some time in the future they would hopefully do missionary work in China. That country, however, was closed to foreign missionaries because of the communist revolution, and it was for this reason that they later decided to volunteer to go wherever they might be needed. They had both been feeling a tug to fulfill the call for missionary service, and the Spirit urged them that this was the time to take their next step.

It would be difficult to leave their pastorate. They had seen the children grow into teenagers, and the teens grow into adulthood. John and Edna had worked with a beautiful group of people whom they had blessed, but they had also been blessed by them! They continued in their pastorate until the North Carolina Annual Conference in 1951.

This camp meeting was a special time for John and Edna. In this conference they were both ordained as missionaries of the Pentecostal Holiness Church. But where would they go? What door would God open for their ministry? They were convinced that the Lord who had called them knew where they could serve Him best.

Rev. W. H. Turner, the Director of Foreign Missions, informed them that Rev. Amos Bradley, a missionary in Costa Rica, had asked for help from the World Missions Board. Brother Bradley had previously gone to Guatemala as a Pentecostal Holiness missionary and served there about 20 years. Along the way, however, he had become disconnected from the Church, but in 1950 he had reestablished his previous commitment. Now he was making a plea for someone to come and help him in the work he had begun in Costa Rica. Would the Parkers be willing to go there? Yes, they would go. Costa Rica, then, would be their first missionary assignment.

Their departure from friends and family came on Christmas Day of 1951. They left amid the tears, good wishes and blessings of the church people, friends, and members of their families. God's call upon their lives was to be realized.

It's never easy to be separated from loved ones, but there is a time and a season for everything, and their time had come to leave kindred and country to follow the leadership of the Lord. They had sung, *Where He leads me, I will follow.* Now, like Abraham, they were going to a country they had never seen and to a nation whose language they could not speak nor understand. But this is the door God had opened, and they would follow.

From North Carolina they drove south to New Orleans, and from there they shipped their car and boarded the plane for Costa Rica.

Costa Rica, land of eternal springtime,
here come the Parkers!

Chapter Three
First Assignment: Costa Rica!

The Parkers arrived in Costa Rica on December 29, 1951. Rev. Bradley met them, and they headed for the valley of Santa Ana where he lived. It was to be their home for a month. Rev. Bradley had worked alone for so many years that he was happy to have new people join him. He took them in as his children, and age-wise, it well could have been. He was 68 and John was 24.

The house was full of people. There was Claudia, the cook and housekeeper with other members of her family. Sigifredo, the chauffer, was also there doing odd jobs. John and Edna felt at home although they didn't understand a word of Spanish.

The next day, Sunday, they were on their way back to San José to the church where they were greeted by about twenty happy, friendly faces. These people were eagerly awaiting their arrival and were introduced as "Don" Juan and "Doña" Edna, the missionaries from the U.S.A. that they had been expecting.

John and Edna surveyed their territory. Rev. Bradley had been there many years, and now he had two small groups meeting in the capital city of San José, one on the north side and another on the south. Together the groups didn't number more than thirty people, and some were taken from one group to the other to have service.

Spiritually Costa Rica was steeped in religion. In the busses almost about all of those on board crossed themselves as they passed a church. On holidays and saints' days, but especially during Holy Week, processions filed through the streets to the sound of mournful dirges. Dedicated people walked miles as they carried their statues through the streets.

None of the evangelical missions seemed to be growing very much, and in the entire nation bornagain believers numbered less than one percent. Evidently their work would not be easy, so there was a big challenge in front of them.

The Parkers spent most of the first year in getting acquainted with the country and its people. They learned early to appreciate the Costa Ricans for who they were—a proud people with a culture and tradition that goes all the way back to the chivalrous days of Queen Isabel's court in old Spain.

After some months of language study that would occupy the entire year, it was possible for

John and Edna to become more active in church work, and they were soon very much involved in the ministry. John's missionary strategy was to follow the pattern set by the Apostle Paul. The Pauline method was first to establish the work in the capital city, go from there to other parts of the urban area, spread out into the small towns, and then to reach out from there to the high mountains, and low jungles.

In the work of reaching the untouched areas, they traveled by plane, car, horse, boat, train, and just walking. It was a challenge. They traveled over paved roads, through grassy lanes, over narrow, rocky paths, and even by slogging along through muddy jungle trails. It was time-consuming travel, but most of the work was in areas where no other church was preaching the gospel.

They learned early that Costa Rica has two principle weather seasons: the rainy season and the dry one. By May the seasonal rains begin, and it would rain just about every day until November. At times, however, these months would be interspersed by heavy downpours (*aguaceros*), and it was then, John said, that they needed to put on their "web feet." By about sundown, the rains would usually stop, and a person could have a bit of time to take care of some necessities. As a pastor who visited his people, the mud was terrible as he went from one small house to the next. But John's reaction was: But all for the glory of God! In one letter he wrote:

I find that when the work is growing and souls are being saved I never notice the inconveniences. It's when things slow up and nothing moves forward that the physical discomforts become more apparent.

They soon established church plants in the metro areas of Heredia and Santa Ana. They were also working with the established churches. In Barrio Cuba and Santa Ana they were struggling to get the people to understand the responsibility and blessing of giving. John gave out tithing envelopes with each person's name, and the people did begin to respond. One man in Santa Ana returned his envelope with ¢3.65 (colons) in it (the equivalent of about 55 cents)!

John also had a burden for the northern jungles of Sarapiquí. His vision was to go in to Puerto Viejo, which is on a navigable river, and from there up to the big San Juan River. His burden was to establish a congregation in this place and work the surrounding areas from there. This goal became a partial reality years later when the church in La Barra was established.

The Parker's work was largely a pioneer one; that is, they were concerned with the tedious and time-consuming task of bringing to full fruition a harvest from the gospel seed they were planting in the hearts of the people. The work of bringing new believers into Christian maturity was actually just as important as getting them saved! Nothing can describe the over-whelming joy or the deep satisfaction that is felt when a soul, overshadowed by darkness and enslaved by false spiritual concepts, comes to the light of the gospel and is set free by a work of the Holy Spirit. As their work progressed, however, the Parkers saw this happen over and over again.

Life has its joys and also its disappointments in the personal life. One of those disappointments was the fact that the Parkers had been married several years, and there had been no babies. On top of this the doctor didn't give them much hope. God has the last word, however, and because He specializes in making possible what seems impossible, He gave them a son. David was born on June 20, 1954, on Father's Day, and just one day before John and Edna's fifth wedding anniversary. They felt that their joy was complete. They were now not just a couple, they were a family! They saw their little boy grow from infancy into early childhood. He didn't know the difference between English and Spanish, but his parents affirm that he never mixed the languages. If you spoke to him in Spanish, he answered in that tongue, or if in English, likewise.

During the first three years in Costa Rica, John and Edna saw three new church buildings go up. They were just hulls, not completed, but they could be used for services. These were tremendously appreciated shelters for people from the heavy downpours of rain. One of their major construction jobs was in Sarapiquí with funds provided by the Bethel North Carolina Church. They finished it inside and out and installed a small generator to provide illumination since there was no electricity in the area. From its beginning the church was alive and growing, and it paid tithes sacrificially toward the support of the work of the Lord.

The Parkers had been in Costa Rica three and one-half years when in April of 1955 Rev. Bradley died of a sudden heart attack. He was 72 years old and had given some 45 years in service as a missionary on foreign soil. The Parkers counted it a privilege and an honor to have worked with him.

Others came to help in the mission work during those early years of the fifties: Floradell Baldwin and Gladys Myrick, both single ladies, were a blessing, but by 1956 both had returned to the United States.

Any Christian worker will at some point ask himself about what kind of results he can see from all he or she is doing. John Parker tells us that it is worth all the work involved! In 1956 he wrote:

> *"I, in company with two other brothers, made a trip into the jungle to visit a home, and we talked to the man there about his spiritual life. He was frankly skeptical, and told us outright that he could not accept a theory or a doctrine unless he saw some manifestation to confirm it.*
>
> *"The man was sick; pale, nervous and frightened. While we talked he was preparing his scheduled dose of medicine, and I put up a detaining hand. 'Friend,' I said, 'wait a moment. Put that medicine to one side for twenty-four hours. We're going to pray for you in the Name of Jesus. If you are not healed in twenty-four hours, take your medicine.' We were putting God to the test, but we believed that He was directing our words.*
>
> *"He followed our suggestion; we prayed that he might be well and left. The next day, we were preparing to board a train eleven miles away,*

*when the healed man walked up having traveled
that distance to tell us that he had seen with his
eyes, and had been touched by the real power of
God. In the service the night before, he had believed."*

Yes, John Parker would tell you, it's worthwhile
to serve even in the most difficult of situations! God
still works miracles to the uttermost!

During this time John established one of his
crowning works—the Bible Institute. He knew that
without trained workers there would be no strong
foundation, so he began the Pentecostal Bible Institute to train ministers. By the end of those first three
years, they had graduated their first three students:
Pedro Murillo, Adán Quesada, and Sigifredo Oroz-
co. These three became strong, faithful pastors, and
year by year new students were added to the educational program.

About a year after the death of Brother Bradley,
Cadell and Vera Ashford arrived from the state of
Virginia, and with their two children they joined
hands with the Parkers. They helped raise money in
order to buy property for the Bible Institute as well
as doing basic church work like planting churches
and serving as pastors and teachers. They helped
train ministers and construct buildings as the meager
funds made that possible. The Parker/Ashford team

entered doors that were opened to them, and they never turned back.

Missionaries, of course, are also just people, and they have problems just like you do. John and David were on their way to a baptismal service in a place called Tabarsia when a drunken doctor crashed into them. David was thrown into the dash and received a nasty cut on his upper lip with lacerations on the inside of his mouth. His gum was chewed badly and his two front teeth were unseated. John only got a few bruises and bumps.

The first and second cars to arrive on the scene were also doctors, and they checked over the hurt ones and arranged to get them to the hospital. David had to have seven or eight stitches in his lip. An hour after they arrived at the hospital, the drunken doctor was brought in by the policeman, and he was still so foggy that an orderly had to walk him up and down the corridor to wake him up! Meanwhile John's car was a mess and uninsured. The doctor fled from the hospital and disappeared. And guess what? John was left on foot!

David was examined by three dentists and two doctors. Officially, his wounds were given two months to heal, and his case would go to a higher court. It would be a long and tedious thing, and John figured that no effort would be made to apprehend the doctor for probably six months.

So, missionaries are just people. They work, but they must also find time to be with family, friends, and the other missionaries. They need to relax, and they have to build into their schedules family and missionary activities to visit the beach, to camp, and to fish—even to go deep-sea fishing when visitors from the States come down! John also had a life-long ambition fulfilled. He learned to fly and got his license. He felt that this could bless the work.

But missionaries also need furloughs from their fields of service. It is a change of scene, a time to visit relatives and friends, and also a time to inform supporting churches about their work.

When John, Edna and David prepared to return to Costa Rica after one furlough, they decided to travel on a shrimping vessel. Why? Well, because it was cheap, and because the ship carried their luggage as well as their car. It certainly wasn't a love boat! Would you ask yourself what it might be like to travel in such a vessel? Well, John wrote his brother during that time:

Dear Wiley,
Just ahead of us, the Gulf turns from its deep blue to an emerald green and breaks across a

long, low, coral reef. A few tufts of land stick up along the horizon...Our boat is a stinking little tub with primitive accommodations, and we have been pretty miserable most of the time...[But] the captain is a first class navigator and has hit his small target head-on every time. We should be back in Costa Rica Thursday morning.

"Bert"

Yes, he was Bert to his family, but to all of his friends and colleagues he was always just John B. Parker. Most of us didn't even know that the "B" stood for Bertram!

In their special activities, a two and one-half week campaign with Rev. Otis Callahan was unforgettable. He ministered in the churches, and people were saved, sanctified and filled with the Spirit. Then they went up to Sarapiquí for services. Three priests there, having heard about their plans. They rode up and down the streets with a loud speaker telling the people not to attend the meetings. At the same time John rode up and down the streets hauling them into the service! After the Sunday morning worship John baptized twenty-one of those people in water!

In the passing of years, Edna never ceased to be a student to better serve the Lord and her husband.

And academically she was awarded her Master of Arts degree in 1967.

The ministry of the Bible Institute can't be over-estimated. From the very beginning, the pastors learned the importance of seeing the Bible as a whole, of studying it, teaching it, and of preaching its truth. Finishing their Bible Institute training was a requirement for ordination, so the students were challenged to get the training.

With time, the more mature ministers graduated, and the newer students who enrolled were younger. It was then that John began to ask himself if the Institute was really fulfilling its mission.

As the years have passed, however, it became clearly evident that the training was not only essential for the development of those young people, but it was also of vast importance for God's Kingdom. Those young people became mature ministers, and they are now leaders in conferences. They are also teachers, missionaries and ministers around the world. Some of the best pastors in the U.S. Hispanic churches are Costa Ricans now serving as pastors, evangelists and leaders of denominational programs.

With the beginning of the Bible Institute, the next great challenge was to find property to construct facilities for the Bible School. It was expected that this property would serve as conference grounds for youth camps, camp meetings and special conventions. It was a pressing need, but nothing is impossible with God. There was a time of waiting, but God changes those impossibilities into the possible!

In 1967 a location was found and purchased in Santa Ana near the metro area of San José, the capital city. It was a five acre tract and a beautiful location facing the east. When the sun rises above the mountains, only the early riser knows the beauty of the sky as God paints it with a myriad of astounding colors.

Two programs were later added to the training: the extension Bible Institute, and CURSUM. The extension program was set up in different churches and made possible the training of people who were not able to leave their homes for the months required at the Bible Institute. This especially met the needs of the older students.

CURSUM (meaning "Advanced Ministerial Training Course") was designed specifically for those who had already graduated from the Bible Institute and wanted to further their education, but it was also for those who were still students in the Institute. Materials were distributed ahead of time, and a week was set aside for this training. Mature teachers were brought to Costa Rica for the week, and most all of the national leaders were trained in these one-week sessions.

Along with Institute responsibilities, missionary work in the churches in the metro and in the country went on. A camper, given to the Parkers by the St Paul Church of Greenville, North Carolina, proved to be a real blessing for the work in the rural districts. To be able to cook, eat, and sleep in one neat little package was so much better than the scattered inconveniences they had previously experienced. It was a real puzzle for the children. They were vitally interested in it and wanted to know if it was a funeral car!

In the summer of 1969 the General Youth Department sent a "Youth in Action Team" to Costa Rica. They would be hosted in the new Bible Institute property. John wrote his brother the following:

Dear Wiley,

I have been rushing around today in last minute details getting things ready for the nine or ten young people who arrive tomorrow at 7:45 from Miami... I have made bunk beds, and bought chairs, and tables. I have tried to get drains and grass in front of the Institute building where they will be staying. It has rained like in the days of Noah every day... and things get pretty sloppy. I think the kids are going to have a problem with flies in the dining room, but I can't put screens over the dorms and windows of the kitchen and dining room until the eaves are closed in... We will have them here for lunch tomorrow. We will start them off with a good meal. Who knows what they will be eating before they leave us!

The young people were chaperoned by Charlene West, a pastor in California, who was recently widowed. They were a great team and ready to do whatever the tasks might be that Brother John might give them to do. Incidentally one of those young people became the General Superintendent of the denomination— Bishop Dr. Douglas Beacham.

So this team was put in the new Bible Institute property. It was a great place to be, but how muddy that road was that led up to it! The young men helped work on that. Charlene West, who had some university training in Spanish, had gone down with two sermon outlines translated into Spanish, but when she was invited to speak a third time to the same congregation, the appearance of "Don Juan" gave instant relief! She was later destined to become a part of the Costa Rican team.

At the end of 1969 and the beginning of 1970 two families came from the U.S. to help in the Bible Institute and to work in other needy areas. James and

Barbara Dickinson, who had served as missionaries in Hawaii arrived with their two children, as well as Charlene West, with three of her four children. She had served as an evangelist and pastor. Although she had studied Spanish she, as well as the Dickinsons, enrolled in the Spanish Language Institute.

The work of these new missionaries was multiple besides teaching and working at the Bible Institute. James was a helping hand to John and Cadell with construction and also keeping the cars running. He could fix a car if nothing but a string, a wire, or a clothes hanger happened to be available to make the repairs! He was also soon up in the river area, where James promoted the work in La Barra del Colorado. You could get there by boat, but you could also fly—if someone on the ground could shoo the pigs, goats and chickens off the only place a plane could land!

James and Barbara Dickinson, along with their work in the metro and in the Bible Institute, were strengthening the work in other areas. Barbara had a burden for the girl's ministry and worked that area on a conference level. She was able to get some of the very basic work translated.

Charlene was soon typing John's Spanish manuscript on the basic doctrines of the Pentecostal Holiness Church (*Doctrinas Básicas*) and before the end of the year she was keeping financial books for the mission and pastoring the church in Barrio Cuba.

Charlene West's teaching and preaching ministry was focused in the power and necessity of the work of the Holy Spirit in the church. A youth revival in Barrio Cuba began and lasted for over a month. Twenty-five were saved and sanctified and thirty received the baptism of the Spirit. Charlene later led that church in the construction of their church building. She was a church planter and went on to begin new works in Alajuelita (when the original work closed) and in Sagrada Familia. She took a home group started by Rev. Pedro Murillo in La Florida de Tibás, organized it, and arranged for the buying of property for their future building.

The tasks were great and the responsibilities were many, but John and Edna, as well as the Ashfords, had gifts of appreciation. Everyone was accepted according to the talents God had given them, and each one felt he or she was important to the work of the team. The fellowship was great.

The MKs (missionaries' kids) made up a team of their own. They were all near the same age. David (known to the missionary family as Davey – but please don't call him that now!) had learned Spanish along with English from birth. Alan and Vera Lynn Ashford over the years had become fluent in the language, but it was different for the other missionary kids. Terri and Karen Dickinson were beginners with the language. The West boys, Joseph and Philip just barely got beyond "sí" and "no," although Kathy had studied a bit in the elementary school before leaving the U.S. These eight however became great friends, and since they all spoke English, they had no language barriers. They all enjoyed Paul West when he could join the MK crowd, when he was out of college classes at vacation time.

It is of vital importance that missionary children be fed spiritually, and it was a little difficult at first when the Dickinson and West children attended services and didn't understand anything at all. The parents and veteran missionaries helped fill in the gaps, however, by teaching them in English. Since their worship and learning at this time in their lives was foundational, their training was of vital importance for the future.

To these MKs John Parker was a man of vision and authority. The guidelines he set were honored, because he was honored and loved.

This same respect was visible among the pastors, leaders and people of the churches. "Don Juan" spoke Spanish better than they did, and he opened new opportunities for them to branch out into unknown areas and plant new churches. He was a spiritual guide and a teacher who faithfully led them by example. He practiced what he preached.

Peru

John was honored in Costa Rica but also in other areas. He was asked to share in a convention sponsored by Charismatic Catholics that was taking place in Lima, Peru. Many people had heard of the event and had traveled long distances to be there for the activity. It was an unforgettable week, and John said that up to that point in time in many ways it was the greatest two weeks he and Edna had ever spent.

This Charismatic retreat was held in a convent with about 200 priests and nuns present plus a few Protestants: a Baptist couple, Methodists, Lutherans, Presbyterians, etc. John and Edna were the only "traditional" Pentecostals in the group. All the Protestants had received the Pentecostal Baptism as well as many of the Catholics. The Mother Superior of the convent was a Spirit-filled woman as well as a priest, George De Prizio who was a gentle and gracious person. These "experts" (as they called them) formed part of the team of counselors, and they ministered as the Lord directed them.

There were many things the Parkers could not exactly relate to from their own background and teachings, but in the midst of it all, they were well aware that God was doing something with those people. John and Edna were assured that God had sent them down there, not only to teach, but also to learn.

On the last night in Lima, they celebrated a Pentecostal service in a great church. It was joyous, spontaneous, and full of the Spirit. In their worship they played guitars, accordions, and tambourines. They sang and prayed in tongues, and they prayed for the sick and for people to receive the baptism of the Spirit.

On to Chimbote after the Lima retreat! It was about 400 miles up the coast where there was a steel mill, about fifty fish fertilizer factories, and a fleet of about 500 boats. It was an interesting trip, and there was a lot to see.

About 75% of the city had been destroyed when it was hit hard the previous year by an earthquake. The women of the team stayed in a school operated by the nuns, and the men were with some priests. John and Edna were personal guests of the Bishop, and he put them up in the best hotel. What a blessing! They were also his guests each day for lunch and dinner, and Ms Edna, with a rose pinned on her dress, was designated to preside over the table for the guests. This was a ministry she carried out with dignity. Her specialty was food and the dinner table!

Argentina

John's ministry was also solicited in other countries. In 1972 he spent six weeks in Argentina preaching and teaching the Word as he coordinated the Bible school work in Buenos Aires.

Mexico

In the same year he was invited to spend a week in Mexico presiding at their annual conference. In 1973 John was the main theological speaker in the King Memorial Lectures. So even from *chica* (little) Costa Rica, the name of John Parker took on a greater meaning.

In Costa Rica the church had been blessed to have the Spanish Language Institute in the nation. The Institute is dedicated to the preparation of those who need the Spanish language to carry on their work. In the past, the majority of the students have been missionaries who plan to work in Spanish-speaking countries. Those of our church who enrolled had been quick to make themselves available to help in the churches—James and Barbara Dickinson, Charlene West, Judy (Firebaugh) Perez; Kaye (Martin) Muñoz; the Eric Vernelsons, and others who studied and helped.

John later wrote about the twenty-three years in Costa Rica that he would always remember.

I remember those years we spent in Costa Rica pioneering the work. I will never forget the hard hours of language study, the exhausting trips to hidden areas where no other preacher had been, the beauty of wild places – mountains, jungles, and ocean. I remember most of all the indescribable look of hunger on their faces and the resultant expression of peace as they found Christ. I recall the great moves of the Spirit as God broke satanic opposition, and scores of people streamed down the aisles in great campaigns. Like a flood it all comes to me.

There came a time however, when John and Edna felt the need to analyze the Costa Rican work force. They had worked in the capital city, in small towns, in the high mountains, and the low jungles. They had trained pastors who had become students of the Word, proficient preachers and competent administrators. The Conference by now was under strong national leadership, and there were missionaries to carry on the work of the Bible Institute. The work had grown over the years, and by this time the work numbered 18 churches and 800 members.

Many different people later would work in Costa Rica and play an important part in the expansion of the work. These people came after John and Edna Parker left, but worked on the firm foundation that the Parkers had laid. They also invested their time, labor, money, and prayers in bringing the work to the place it is today with approximately 80 churches and over 15,000 members.

From their standpoint, however, the Parkers believe that the real heroes of the Costa Rican story are the national brothers and sisters who have invested themselves in bringing the work where it is today. They have sacrificed, suffered and given their lives in building the IPHC in Central America. These: the Parkers, their fellow missionaries and their faithful pastors together have been church planters, cultivators, trainers, teachers, and encouragers, but it is always God who has given the increase.

John and Edna realized that the national leaders had become capable of directing conference administration, and they saw them elected and installed in the work of the conference while they were still on the field. At that time there was also a good team teaching the Institute curriculum. The Parkers felt their time in Costa Rica was finished, and that it was time for capable nationals that John had trained to take the lead and carry on. John discerned that his time in Costa Rica was finished. He and Edna were now looking forward to working with different Bible schools on different fields.

The General Lifeliners (Youth) Department had purchased a new pick-up with a shell, and the Parkers were to drive it down. This was to be a great blessing to the work for missionaries often had to take supplies with them for constructions as well as to stay overnight. It was a vehicle that could be very adaptable to the needs of the mission. The Parker's stay this time, however, was to be short, because John had accepted a job at Southwestern College in Oklahoma City.

There was a feeling of sadness, of course, as the Parkers prepared to leave Costa Rica. They had worked with these people for many years and they loved them. They had married many of the young couples, dedicated their babies to the Lord, seen the children grow up and take their places in life. They felt, however, that the Lord was speaking to them to move on, and they were confident that the work they had begun would continue to go forward. Seed that is planted will continue to bear fruit.

The Costa Rican brothers, along with missionaries Cadell and Vera Ashford, Charlene West, and James and Barbara Dickinson would continue what the Parkers had started. They felt good about leaving the work in the very capable hands of these servants of the Lord.

In his journal John noted that in the five and one-half years between 1967 and 1972, there was a 140% member increase, because the Lord added to the church those who were receiving Him. It was an encouraging gain! In addition, from the Costa Rican work churches have been planted in Nicaragua, Honduras, Panama, and Belize. The efforts of the good leadership and faithful workers surely had made an impact that reached into other countries of the world!

Years later in May of 1982 John and Edna were privileged to return to Costa Rica for the first time after leaving eight years previously. What a joy it was for them to visit this city again and see so many of their friends who had been faithful through the years. It was also a blessing to visit the churches where they had previously labored for twenty-three years. How encouraging it was to see the revival and growth the Costa Rican church was enjoying! Surely the Parkers had planted the seed, God had sent the rains, and others were there to see that the harvest was brought in. God was using those faithful men and women who realized that it was only in the power and might of the Holy Spirit that they were able to see the work move forward.

John Parker

They had planted seed that had brought forth fruit, some thirty, some sixty and some even one hundred fold. God is faithful to send the rains of the Spirit so that the harvest can grow and be multiplied.

The workers had been faithfully trained, and they remembered and ministered in the power of the Holy Spirit!

It's not by might nor by power,
but by My Spirit, says the Lord of hosts!
Zechariah 4:6

Chapter Four
From the Classroom to Hong Kong!

The plane that took John and Edna Parker from San José, Costa Rica landed in the Atlanta, Georgia airport. Their son, David, met them and drove them to Franklin Springs, Georgia where they rented one of the "Madrid" apartments. (Little did they realize that fourteen years later they would actually be renting and living in Madrid, Spain!)

They had very little with which to start keeping house. Fortunately the kitchen was furnished, and they looked for odds and ends to fill in the gaps. A card table served for dining, and two camp stools became their chairs and foot stools. A small antique chair that had belonged to Edna's grandfather helped complete the picture, and they tried to make the place as attractive and comfortable as possible with their few belongings.

John decided that the first piece of furniture they needed to buy was a color TV, since they had never had one. Their friends, Karl and Lois Bunkley, thought it quite amusing to find them sitting on the floor, watching TV, and eating off a card table! But they were happy, as they knew they were following the Lord and that things would soon improve.

From Georgia they went on to Oklahoma City, Oklahoma to begin teaching at Southwestern College (later named Southwestern Christian University). It was a new beginning for the Parkers. It seemed strange not to be a part of the World Missions Department of the church, since that had been their work connection for years. At Southwestern John was an instructor in American History, Evangelism, the Four Gospels, and Missions. Edna taught Spanish at Southwestern and also in the public schools of Oklahoma City.

In his second year at Southwestern, John was asked to become Dean of the School of Religion, the area of the school that granted degrees in Theology, Christian Education, Music, and Missions. From the early years as a student at Holmes and East Carolina, John knew that education was of great importance for the minister of the Gospel. He felt, therefore, that in this Christian institution he was fulfilling a very specific need in the training of Christian ministers.

In this setting, John was privileged to have interchange with people who were not only professors, but who were also deep thinkers. John was working with people like James Gamble, James Taylor, Paul

Oxley, Doug Barton, Noel Brooks, and others. It was stimulating not only intellectually, but also spiritually, to be able to have fellowship with these great men of the Word.

John and Edna were comfortable. They liked their work, and they had bought a house. Their son, David, had married a dedicated young lady, Irvina Smith, and at this time they lived nearby. As John taught his students on the challenge of world missions, however, there came over him a vague sense of restlessness. He remembered the strength of his own call and the feeling that he would reach people in other nations of the world. He also remembered his work in Costa Rica. It had been difficult at times; there had been long exhausting trips to remote areas of the country. At times growth had been slow, and they had also faced satanic opposition. Yet it had been worthwhile.

He had invested himself in people who would keep on reaching the lost in places where he could no longer go. He had seen God move first hand on the mission field and change lives. Although he realized that what he was doing now was important, he asked himself about those "regions beyond" where perhaps others would not go. If he didn't continue to carry the torch, who would? He had heard the call, *Whom shall I send? Who will go for Us?* He had answered, but had he truly fulfilled that call? Why was the burden still there?

Early in December of 1978 John lifted the telephone receiver expecting nothing more than a casual call from David or from some friend. Classes were over for the day, and he was ready to unwind. It was the voice of the World Missions Director, B. E. Underwood, however, that came through. His greeting was short, as usual, and he came through with a question that shook John up: *"How soon can you and Edna be in Hong Kong?"* His thoughts raced into high gear!

"What do you mean—Hong Kong?" John had visited Hong Kong three years previously, and the crowded city had almost overwhelmed him.

"Well," Rev. Underwood replied, *"the Board would like very much for you and Edna to move to Asia as our new supervisors of that area."*

They agreed to talk the next day over coffee, and something in John's voice elicited a groan from Edna, *"Uh-oh, here we go again!"* It sounded like a change was on the way.

When a decision had been reached and all had been settled according to the wishes of World Missions Director B. E. Underwood, he spoke to his staff of workers. He wanted to introduce the newest members on the staff:

I am so happy to welcome John and Edna Parker to our staff. They will be stationed in Hong Kong for the present, and Brother Parker will be filling the gap in Hong Kong while our field superintendent, Sherrill Orvin, is on furlough. He will also be spending some time giving guidance to other areas. It is a real source of strength to be able to add a man of Brother Parker's ability and skills to our missionary staff. I appreciate his deep dedication to missions.

And so to Asia John and Edna went. She may have groaned at the thought at first, but her commitment as always was to John. *Wherever you go, John, I will go!* And so they went. On the day of their departure from Oklahoma City, the Muse Memorial Church gave them a farewell service in which church and missions officials laid hands on them and sent them forth to their new ministry in the Far East.

Their fast-paced trip began after the hectic days of sorting, storing, and packing, but they carried in their hearts the good-byes and good wishes of so many dear friends, and they loved them for it. They spent a short two nights in Los Angeles visiting John's brother, followed by a stop in Honolulu with a refreshing time of fellowship with Mrs. Mildred Brostek, a dynamic church planter there. They also

enjoyed uplifting moments with the church people in
Kailua while eating a meal with the Yuens and
McCalls. How wonderful it was to have friends!
Then they were soon "on board" again, however, to
continue their journey.

From Hawaii their twelve-hour flight finally
came to an end. At last it was a reality. They were on
the continent of Asia in the city of Hong Kong. The
city is a vast mosaic of nations, cultures, tongues,
and contradictions. At that time it had a population
of five and one-half million people. It presented an
immense and mammoth challenge to the faith of
John and Edna, but they knew they had the prayers
of many people behind them!

They looked back to their days of study at
Holmes Bible College and remembered that their
challenging missionary calls had first come to them
to go to China. And now here they were, right on the
doorstep of China, the land of their original calling.
When God speaks, He makes no mistakes. There
may be a time of waiting and challenge as God's
people are involved in other tasks, but God makes no
mistakes. He is faithful to fulfill His Word.

Hong Kong was to be their base as they reached
out into other parts of Asia. This city is called the
Pearl of the Orient, and John and Edna felt it lived
up to its exotic name. As missionaries on a new as-

signment, they felt the need of spiritual assurance. They were welcomed by the missionaries and Chinese people, and they found special blessing in the Wednesday and Saturday prayer meetings. Certainly these came to be times of fellowship and spiritual nourishment.

So many things, however, were different—even shopping for food. Nearly everything was imported coming in tightly closed packages usually frozen or sterilized. Soon, however, they were using chopsticks like veterans, and they grew to love the place with all of its bigness.

In spite of many battles against the forces of the enemy, the Christian people had stood strong, and there was so much to appreciate. The most fascinating fact was that there was a solid Pentecostal Holiness Church, born and nurtured over 75 years. Dedicated pastors, leaders and Christian families had proven themselves faithful, and they had been victorious over typhoons, war, famine, and the shadowy threat of the communist invasion. But God's work had moved forward, and it had stood the test of time. God's people who are wholly committed to Him have at their disposal all of heaven's resources.

In Hong Kong John and Edna were able to feel the pulse of the surrounding areas as they oversaw the work of the church. John was soon deep in the business affairs of the work—making decisions on buying, selling, and building. More important, however, was that God's Word was going forth and many people were yielding their lives in repentance and service to Christ. In the spirit, John and Edna both vibrated with an intense desire to see a powerful move of God among the pastors and churches.

One morning the words of the song, How Great Thou Art kept flooding John's mind, and he was reminded of something he had recently read:

When we are caught up with the greatness of God, we don't ask for the pennies in His hand, because we have His hand. When we have His hand, we don't need answers, because He is the Answer.

Sometimes the Parkers were required to make trips to the U.S. to enlist additional support, and they held to the words found in Joshua 1:9, "...*For the Lord our God will be with you wherever you go.*" On one occasion they squeezed in a few days to get acquainted with their first grandchild, little David Ryan.

Do you wonder what these missionaries do while they have furloughs or make other necessary trips to the U.S.? John wrote after spending four months in the United States:

While at home Edna and I told our "missions" story in 25 churches, attended two World Missions Board meetings, took part in the annual School of Missions, enjoyed the C. E. Convention in Orlando, and rejoiced in a five-day Missions Convention with George Bass in St. Augustine. We also stopped two times with Bill Wilson and his California people. We had great fellowship and victory in the Word.

Just before returning to Hong Kong, they were privileged to visit the church in Rocky Mount, North Carolina where they both held their church membership. It was in this church that John had been saved so many years before.

How they appreciated the many across the nation who had made financial commitments of faith and had consistently contributed to their work in the "regions beyond." In their correspondence and newsletters, they always added their words of appreciation.

We thank you from our hearts for your giving, prayers and interest in us and in our ministry. Your faithfulness will be remembered by our God who keeps exact records.

Then it was back on the plane headed for Hong Kong. They leaped the mighty ocean, almost in a single bound, and touched down briefly in Honolulu. Back in Hong Kong, John's pace was accelerated as he made visits to other countries and cared for things under his direction in the city. While there he spent his time in church services, board and committee meetings, checking on the construction of the new seventeen-story Shaukiwan building and making plans for the coming year.

John and Edna were impressed by the multi-faceted work in Hong Kong. The ministry not only ministered to spiritual needs of the people, but also to the handicapped and hurting. For example they saw the Center for the Blind grow and expand. It had previously been a meeting place for a few elderly people, but soon they saw it take on new enthusiasm. A dozen or more newly-converted young people became a part of this ministry, and it was touching to see the compassion and care that these young people gave to the aged and handicapped. They had found a need and filled it!

At the close of the year, John and Edna visited the Saam Mun Tsai kindergarten where 109 lovely Chinese children reenacted the Christmas story. Then the children gave the Parkers an extra thrill; they wanted them to pose with them for a picture!

The hearts of John and Edna yearned for revival in the churches, and they were visionaries. They had faith that it would happen, and that they could be a part of it. The Parkers were always glad to have their church officials visit them. They, also, were visionaries!

Rev B. E. Underwood, the World Missions' director, and Bishop Leon Stewart, the general superintendent of the Pentecostal Holiness Church, visited them. They had a heavy schedule of five sessions each day of teaching and worship. Twenty leaders attended in Hong Kong, but together they went from the base city to the regions around them to teach in seminars. Thirty of their leaders attended the sessions in Madras and fifty in North India. They saw a deep interest on the part of the people, and together they enjoyed times of prayer and glorious fellowship. At the end of these full days there was no need for lullabies to put them to sleep in the evening!

One of the Chinese pastors in Hong Kong, along with a group of his church members, made an extensive trip into Mainland China with the plan of making contacts for future Christian service. The Hong Kong church was helping get Bibles into China! John thanked the Lord for the good Christian witness in Hong Kong, but he always asked the people to remember to pray for the millions of Chinese people who were still unreached!

John never forgot his early call or his training to reach the world with the gospel. His perspective from Hong Kong would be giving him an opportunity, not only to reach and teach those in that great international city, but also to reach the nations around him. As has already been projected, he and Edna worked as a team. John was more up front, but Edna was always at his side partnering with him. She was a blessing not only to the work, but also to the individual ministry of John. Her never-failing sense of humor, her ministry of hospitality, and her words of encouragement were and would continue to be a tremendous blessings to John's ministry. When he chose Edna as his life's partner, he had chosen well.

It was from the tremendous base in Hong Kong that John and Edna would be able to extend themselves into other regions of the world around them.

Chapter Five
From the Base to Other Nations

As one New Year was ushered in, John and Edna took as theirs the promise the Lord made to
Joshua: *...for the Lord your God will be with you
wherever you go* (Joshua 1:9).

The Parkers officially resided in Hong Kong, but
their life was made up of "comings and goings."
They shuttled across the oceans, went from one continent to another, and traversed the nations as they
answered the Master's call to the harvest. From
Hong Kong they were continually challenged by the
nations around them. Just beyond them were the un-
evengelized millions of Asia.

Mainland China:

John's first visit to Mainland China was a highlight among his missionary experiences. He counted
this tour, not only a great opportunity, but also the
fulfillment of a call. The vision of missions that God
had originally placed on his heart many years pre-

viously had been a vision of China. To visit that country would indeed be a blessing if he could fulfill a need in so doing.

China! A vast land of one billion people at that time! During twelve days of his visit he was in the cities of Buangzhou, Kweilin, Changsa, Beijing, and Shanghai. He was bombarded with powerful and strange impressions while he tried to mentally put it all together. There were so many things to see: there were cities and communes, palaces and people, factories and farms, and a nation trying desperately to modify its direction after thirty years of Marxism and Mao.

He also saw churches, only a few, but he thanked God for them. He talked to Christians who were eager to share their faith and express their gratitude to God for a bit of relaxation on the part of an atheistic government. John's clarion call was, "Pray for China!" The Chinese believe that God can and will do an unbelievable work there in the coming years, and they are deeply grateful for those who are hearing and sharing their call for prayer.

John took another trip into China and was able to make the trip both ways by train. His special purpose was to take in a heavy load of Bibles to be distributed to Chinese Christians.

Edna's heart also became burdened with the need
to get God's Word into the hearts of the Chinese.
She became engaged in a very special ministry with
five other ladies, and together they also made a trip
to the Mainland. They were not so blessed as to be
able to go in by train. They traveled in an overnight
boat up the Pearl River, during which time she and
two of the ladies shared their cabin with a Chinese
man!

At Canton in Mainland China, they took in a
large number of Bibles as well as gospel portions to
be distributed among the Chinese Christians. Bibles
were desperately needed as the following prayer request from the Christians in Henan, China indicates:

> *Ask the Lord to give us more Bibles, so that all
> who yearn after His word may have it. Please
> pray for China!*

Tibet

John also took a trip into "forbidden Tibet," so
called because it is a place where few at that time
were allowed to enter. Tibet is indeed the "roof of
the world." Llasa, its capital city, is at about
15,000 feet in altitude. Tourists have to have a
heart and lung exam in order to make the trip. As
a place, Tibet is lonely, isolated, ancient, and oc-

cupied by Chinese armies. It is a land of monks and monasteries, prayer wheels and pagodas, yaks and friendly people. Their religion is a poisonous brand of Buddhism, laced with demon and devil worship that enslaves three million people. It is a land of deep darkness. Our group of 19 Christians left forty copies of the Tibetan Bible in the hands of the temple priests with the firm faith that God can use His Word to bring forth belief and salvation.

In spite of everything negative, John found the grace of God there. High on a hill overlooking Llasa, they found a cross. Who knows what brave, courageous group of believers had dared to defy this hard religion with its despotic political power to place that cross there? Whoever they were, they needed and deserved our prayers and intercession.

Korea

John and Edna went to Korea, a country known for war, destruction, and reconstruction, as well as for some of the Kingdom's greatest revivals. John had already visited Korea and preached four nights with great victory in the church pastored by Rev. Jung Whan Kim. At that time John was able to visit with Rev. James Gamble with whom he had had fellowship while teaching at Southwestern College.

A church had given the Parkers money to buy an electric oven for the Gambles, and they were anxious to get it to them. The Lord had laid it on Edna's heart while in the U.S. to take this oven to Korea for the Gambles. Bertha Gamble only had two small gas burners for a stove! Sometimes the Korean government charges 100% or more as duty, and Edna had earnestly prayed that they would be able to take the oven in without duty. As the large box with the oven came off the luggage belt, she laid her hands on it again and prayed,

Now, Lord, I have asked You before, but again I ask that there be no duty on this gift.

The inspector asked all kinds of questions about the box. He didn't seem to understand what it was and even after seeing the picture on the box, he couldn't figure it out. He kept saying that it was a very expensive item. Three others came with their opinions, and they came up with the sum of $75. John told them that they were asking too much, and that they would pay $20. Immediately the officer told them that they could go. John reached for the money, but the man motioned them on their way. They left praising the Lord for answering prayer! They had paid no duty on the item! Zero dollars! God is still in the business of answering prayer!

The next day, they took a four-hour bus ride up to the town nearest the Gambles residence. From there it was a taxi ride on up the muddy mountainous road to the top. It was like Christmas for Bertha Gamble when she saw that oven! And, you guessed it, the first thing she did was to bake a cake for the Parkers! This was Bertha's way of showing her appreciation for this gift. Missionaries always find a way to bless and take care of one another!

Afterward, they were with the Gambles for the annual open-air camp meeting on the mountain (although they had to move inside later because of the unseasonal rains).The rains, however, didn't keep the people from getting up at 4:30 in the morning to pray all over that mountain! They believe that all things can be resolved by prayer. What faith!

On the following Sunday John and Edna attended the church that Rev. Cho pastors along with some 12,000 others, not counting the thousands standing in the rain to attend the next service. Knowing that we have a great big God, they prayed that God would multiply churches like these throughout the world. They are needed to be able to reach multitudes like these in Korea who had come to know the King of kings! Surely nothing is impossible with God!

India:

Exotic India stole their hearts completely for everything was unique in this ancient land of paradoxes. They plowed their fields as Abraham and his neighbors did, and yet they could lift satellites into space! John and Edna tried their spicy, pungent food, smelling of cardamom, cinnamon, turmeric, and hot peppers. It excited their appetites—no doubt about it. The fellowship of missionaries like the Howards, the Donalds, Frances Carter and Louise Smith made every visit memorable. Ministry among our fine workers in both North and South India became challenging and rewarding.

On one special occasion John, Kenneth Donald and the South India Superintendent went to Madras to make plans for a church to be planted by the "Operation Antioch" program. The vision was to plan for a church of 4,000 members during the following four years. The pastor, Rev. Vidyasagar had already raised up about 450 people from several different groups of baptized Christians. Twenty-five of these were selected leaders for special training as home-cell leaders.

India has specialized in establishing hostels to give assistance to needy children. It was a blessing when Rev. James Pennington came and reviewed our People-to-People Program that ministers to children around the world with food, clothing, and educational needs.

On one occasion, John rode an overnight train for sixteen hours to reach the crowded and dusty town of Maruter. There they had three days of glorious worship and ministry with our missionaries and workers of the Andhra Conference. John was invited to give a seminar in Bihar and in the twenty-fifth year Jubilee celebrations in Andhra Pradesh. He also helped in the shooting of 30 roles of video film to give people in the U.S. an idea of the work in India.

There were notes of sadness, however, because one of their most honored partners was no longer with them. In one correspondence, John wrote:

We had fellowship with our missionaries, Joan Donald and Frances Carter, and with our superintendent, Rev. Vidyasagar. How strongly we felt the absence of our dear Ken Donald, who went to heaven in August past.

Philippines

Plans were activated to establish a center in Manila for the training of urban pastors, and John saw this center become operational through funds received from the U.S. Plans for a second center were set in motion for the Igorot tribes-people of Northern Luzon.

John and Edna continually express their thankfulness for the generosity of their friends and Christian brothers in the homeland. Without them, their prayers and their support, it would be impossible for them to move forward.

What great blessings they received through the ministry of Rev. John Hedgepeth when he came for a visit. He shared his ministry in four seminars, and the faith of the people was lifted up as he challenged them to believe God for great and mighty things. Only those missionaries who are working in the harvest know the joy and blessings that are received through those who come and bring with them "showers of blessing" in the power of the Holy Spirit.

Bill and Bette Anderson arrived in the Philippines to begin their ministry on the big island of Mindanao. The Parkers were joyfully anticipating a rich harvest of souls and much church planting to come from their labors. Bill has a track record, not only as a pastor, but also as a builder. So he was soon involved in the ministry of the Word, but also in new constructions. On one occasion John wrote:

This week we go to the Philippines to see what God is doing there. The new church, Grace Chapel, is nearing completion in Manila, and our Bible School students are as busy as bees spreading the Word in new areas.

About another trip he wrote: *In Davao City, we inspected the seven church buildings which Bill Anderson has under construction. Some were nearby; others were 75 miles away.*

The next Sunday in Toril, during church services a shoot-out occurred between the government marines and a guerrilla group. Ten people were killed; three of them were innocent civilians. The missionaries were unaware of the problem until the next day.

In spite of the blessing Bill and Bette Anderson were for the work and the construction of so many church buildings for worship, by October 1984 they were forced out of Mindanao because of extortion threats. We were all deeply grateful for the Andersons' contributions to the work in the Philippines.

Indonesia:

In February of 1982, John ministered for three days to a group of pastors in Indonesia who became the first Pentecostal Holiness witness in that island nation of 140 million people.

It was a blessing for the Parkers to have Rev. B.E. Underwood, the World Missions Director, and Bishop Leon Stewart with them for a special service to welcome these Christian brothers into our fellowship. Bishop Stewart preached in a special service that evening. Their party left the hotel at 8:30 to ride 40 miles into the countryside. The rural dirt roads led them through plantations of bananas and palm nut trees to finally reach a church where 150 people waited for the preaching of the Word. At 11:30 P.M. the missionaries were seated on the floor of a deacon's house eating a late meal of rice and curry. They got back to their hotel at 1:00 A.M.!

On a later date John and Rev. James Pennington held a five-day seminar in Medan for twelve churches and their pastors. God blessed them in the riverside baptismal service where 29 new believers confirmed their faith in Christ as Lord of their lives. Other activities included an open-air village meeting, and then a visit to minister pray in a colony of lepers.

John then had seminars planned for Indonesia, Hong Kong, and the Philippines where he visited several new churches that had just opened up on the island of Bohol. Edna then joined him for a six day visit to India where he presided over the election of the Conference Board. Four days later, they left for

London where John would be teaching for two weeks.

During his stay in London, John made a weekend trip to Paris riding trains and a ferry from London. Exactly forty years previous to that day, the Channel had been choked with three thousand ships preparing for D-Day. John remembered well that morning. His Dad had gotten up early as usual, and turned on the radio, and the news began filtering in that the landings had begun. For many, those times seem like ancient history, but to those who were close to the scene of action, and to those who could only wait and pray, that time will never be forgotten. The day John was there, however, the northern shores of France were quiet—all except for the hum of commerce and the coming and goings of tourism.

During this time Rev. John Hedgepeth, pastor of Northwood Temple in Fayetteville, North Carolina visited the Parkers and wrote about the wonderful time he had enjoyed with them:

I was overwhelmed with my visit to the Philippines and Hong Kong. I feel like you went out of your way to make it one of the highlights of my life. I enjoyed the Philippines... and Hong Kong.

It was time for another furlough for the Parkers, and it was John's habit to analyze what had been done while they had been working. As has been mentioned, he kept a daily journal of his activities. He remembered that in one of the years he had spoken in two graduation ceremonies with 27 graduates in one area and ten in another. On a more global basis, He reported that in the eight years they had been in Asia, the Asian membership through the grace of God, had grown from eight thousand to over seventeen thousand.

John's leadership was recognized and deeply appreciated by those involved in general church work as well as pastors, their supporters and many friends.

Pastor Hedgepeth wrote:

John and Edna, I am amazed at the tremendous leadership you have given our Missions Department...Your leadership...stands out. I know the Lord knows who the real leaders are. Thanks for being you.

At the close of one year during this time, John and Edna put into writing a "thank you" note for what the Lord had done in their lives during that year. God had urged them to *give thanks in everything,* and they were indeed grateful for God's abundant blessings. They wrote right out of their hearts to their many friends as they sent their greetings that year. In reality, a similar note could have been written at the end of any year!

This year will soon be history and such a great year it has been, and to God be the glory! We give Him thanks for:

- Sending Christ Jesus as our Savior
- Saving us and calling us to His service
- Giving us to each other so many years ago
- Allowing us to have a wonderful son and daughter-in law
- Giving us love and acceptance among our fellow missionaries and Chinese Christians
- Seeing the Holy Spirit in operation on our mission fields here in Asia
- Supplying urgent funds for our Bible Schools in the Philippines through our churches here in Hong Kong
- Your faithful giving each month so that we can spread the Good News
- Praying friends like you who seem to know the times we need prayer most
- Faithful working missionaries and nationals who carry a heavy load for the advancement of God's Kingdom

- Permitting us to represent you and the Pentecostal Holiness Church on the mission fields for these many years

When they began to "count their blessings," their list just kept growing. It could have gone on and on, but John and Edna indicated that these were just a few of the most important items for which they wished to say "Thank You" to the God of their salvation!

They had thoroughly enjoyed their work in Hong Kong and in the surrounding areas. They had gone to so many different countries and areas that they had not previously known. They had taught the Word, preached, and ministered. They had prayed with the people and seen God move. They had become acquainted with so many different cities and met so many new friends and workers in God's Kingdom.

When people have unique ministries, however, they are often sought to meet specific needs at certain times. Maybe an organizer is needed to help get a work on a solid foundation. Perhaps a person capable of solving a problem of personnel is sought. At times works need to be analyzed to see what it is doing and how it can become more productive.

John Parker was such a person, and perhaps it has been for this reason that he has been asked to do so many different tasks in so many different places. Perhaps there is no other missionary who has been asked to go to so many different countries because there was a specific need for his unique ministry.

In spite of the fact that John and Edna were enjoying their work in Hong Kong and would have been very happy to stay, that was not to be. God had other plans, because a need for John's unique ministry of teaching had presented itself.

Chapter Six
From Asia back to Latin America

The Parkers were on furlough. On May 16 they flew in to Atlanta and went on to Fayetteville, NC the same day. John was taking an extension course from Fuller Theological Seminary and had loads of work, so he spent a lot of time at the typewriter. He was always busy reading, studying and writing.

Some time ago, John wrote the little book, *Basic Doctrines* of the Pentecostal Holiness Church. It is a very well written and clear presentation of the basic doctrines, not just of the church, but of God's Word. It is now being used in different parts of the world as a very wonderful and tremendous teaching tool. At one point Missions Director B. E. Underwood wrote:

Your book on the basic doctrines in Spanish has been reprinted (1,000 copies). We are contacting June to find out just how she plans to make these available to the Bible schools in Latin America.

71

So John's time at the typewriter proved to be a tremendous blessing for the preparation of those who were serious about their own ministerial training in God's Word. A few days after arriving in North Carolina, John wrote again:

> *On the 20th I am flying down to Santiago, Chile to speak a few times at the Pentecostal Bible Institute and to assess the situation for the Missions Department. This is a joint venture between the Assemblies of God and the Pentecostal Holiness Church, and it is designed to give Bible training to the many indigenous Pentecostal pastors in that country. Already they have 300 enrolled. I understand that they have been asked to train many public school teachers in basic Bible knowledge because the government wishes to teach religion in the schools.*

They were moving again! For the seventh time in their married life, they would set up housekeeping and start with almost nothing. So they packed their bags and boxes and transferred to Chile to become a part of the Pentecostal Bible Institute. They were going back to Latin America where kingdom growth was sweeping the whole continent in unprecedented measure. Their ministry now would be a very literal fulfillment of the Lord's words, *Go ye into all the world and make disciples of all nations, teaching them...*

The Parkers understood that missionaries are soldiers. They are called to a work and not necessarily to a place. And there is always the World Missions Board who can, as they understand the will of God, move the missionaries about. So even as they continued their duties as supervisors of Asian ministries, the Parkers moved to Chile. Missions Director B. E. Underwood wrote:

> *Rev. John Parker, who has served faithfully and well for several years as Asian Supervisor, is now working at the Pentecostal Bible Institute in Santiago, Chile. He and Edna are making a very vital contribution to that large institution for the training of Pentecostal pastors in Chile.*

The Parkers left for Chile on Wednesday, July 9. Their plane flew direct from Miami to Buenos Aires where they were on the ground about an hour and a half. They then crossed over the Andes Mountains to Santiago. Santiago! It is a sprawling city between three and four million people. There are a few tall buildings, but nothing like Hong Kong. There are also many old and poorly maintained cars plus a lot of busses that create a cloud of smog contaminating the air of the city most of the time. Paul Hoff, director of the Pentecostal Bible Institute (PBI), and Dean Helland, one of the professors, were there to meet them.

So the Parkers were back in Latin America—in Chile, called the "shoestring republic," on the western shores of South America. Familiar sounds from the past were all around them: the musical tones of the Spanish language, the sound of the church bells, the guitars, tambourines, and the marimbas. They enjoyed the enthusiastic singing and church worship of the people, because it gave evidence to the great Pentecostal move that was leading the way in gospel preaching and church growth.

But the missionaries there had things ready for them, and it was great to be able to move into the apartment prepared for them by Paul and Betty Hoff. They also felt grateful to Dean and Penny Helland for the valuable orientation they had given them. What a help it proved to be while they were learning their way around this city of three million people. It wasn't as hectic or as crowded as Hong Kong, but it was a man-sized challenge nevertheless.

They had soon set up house, completed their residence documents, bought a small Peugeot auto (supplied by the Missions Department), and purchased a fine IBM typewriter all while getting acquainted with the city.

John and Edna found their way around as they settled in. They tried out the subway and checked out the markets. There was plenty of food—all home-grown, different in packaging and display. Very little food there was imported, and that was very different from Hong Kong where so much *was* imported. Duty was high, so imported stuff would be too expensive to buy. There was a 20% sales tax on everything, even on books.

Their appliances, all used, were expensive, and just the basics cost them $2,500. But the Lord supplied the need, as He always does! A tax refund from Uncle Sam, and a bond bought years ago matured and came just at the right moment.

The climate changes took some adjustments. The July 100° degree heat wave of North Carolina had given way to the frigid winter weather of the Southern Hemisphere. What a change! They took sweaters and topcoats, an electric blanket for the bed, and a small gas heater to take the chill off the air. There was snow on the mountains out of their back window.

John and Edna attended the Jotabeche Pentecostal Methodist Church on their first Sunday. The attendance of 1,500-2,000 grouped itself together in the main sanctuary into smaller groups of ten to fifteen, and it seemed that an invisible wall went up around each segment. The general murmur of noise was evidently tuned out while each group concentrated on its leader. Different? The Parkers thought so, but the method was evidently effective because the people kept coming back! That Sunday John was invited by Bishop Vazquez to address the entire assembly.

In the evening, John preached to a congregation of about 800 at the church in San Bernardo, south of Santiago. Harmonious music came from an orchestra of guitars, accordions, violins, tambourines and reed flutes. It was straight from the heart and straight from Chilean culture. Repeated triple shouts of *"Gloria a Dios"* (Glory to God) punctuated the worship from beginning to end. John wrote about the receptivity of the Chilean people:

> *People have been kind and receptive. The Chileans are warm, emotional, and are great huggers and kissers. I was kissed at least 150 times last night—by old grizzled men, gracious old ladies, young men, and pretty young girls—all in "el Nombre del Señor" (the Name of Jesus).*

Over all this phenomenal church growth and enthusiastic worship, however, there hung a somber cloud that only God could dispel. Hundreds of pastors and thousands of believers there seemed to have little solid knowledge of the Word of God. A long bias against educating preachers had kept them just preaching their personal experiences. With the help of the Lord, John and Edna believed that they could help change this situation. They were committed to making a difference!

On March 14, 1987 the Pentecostal Bible Institute (PBI) opened its doors and rang the bells to signal the beginning of its ninth year of teaching, imparting what the Apostle Paul called "the unsearchable riches of Christ." Every course was designed to prepare pastors and lay-people for some phase of gospel ministry. This year they had enrolled 340 students from 80 different Pentecostal groups. Many were pastors of large and growing churches.

For example there was Marcelo, a third-year student. He had a shoe shine stand in a busy downtown street that had become his pulpit. Urbane and prosperous business men stood in line to have Marcelo talk to them and pray with them about their problems – business, personal, and family needs. Then there was Francisco Orellana, another student, who was planting a new church in a crowded community within sight and smell of a garbage dump!

You can get a glimpse of the Parker's regular work schedule from this paragraph taken from a very interesting newsletter:

John taught eight-week courses on the Life of Christ, 1 Corinthians, Basic Theology, and the Pentateuch. He taught an all-day seminar to a group of 25 pastors and taught a study on the Holy Spirit for four nights in a local church. Edna has taught an eight-week course to a group of ladies on Character study in the book of Genesis.

John and Paul Hoff traveled to Valparaíso (75 miles away) for eight consecutive Saturdays to teach in their first extension school. John felt he had never taught such an enthusiastic group of students as that class of 20 pastors and another of 45 laypeople. One pastor reported that for the first time in his life he had spent four consecutive hours in independent Bible study. Several ladies got so excited about the Word of God that they stayed awake all night discussing what they had learned.

The missionary wives were at work. Erica Grace, Penny Helland, and Edna designed special teaching sessions for the women of local churches, and the response was overwhelming. Over 200 churches accepted applications to be involved in that ministry. As a result they gave 325 certificates to all the ladies who had perfect attendance in their classes.

Meanwhile John continued to travel. During this time he went to Costa Rica and also to Venezuela teaching CURSUM (advanced ministerial) classes. In Costa Rica an estimated 700 people attended the first CURSUM graduation. John recently preached to large congregations of several thousand and to a small beginning church of 35 meeting in the open air. Four people came to the Lord in that humble service.

John and Edna, however, were not destined to continue the work in Chile. They would be moving again! But of their ministry in Chile, John wrote:

What a privilege it has been to know this lovely country with its kind and receptive people! And how good to have known and worked with the staff and students of the Pentecostal Bible Institute, to have had a small part in shaping the minds, the hearts, and the character of our students as they prepare for ministry to their own people. The Pentecostal pastors and churches of Chile have provided us with great fellowship and high moments of inspiration. Unique in many ways, they are a prime example of what a witnessing church should be. Our relationship with Bishop Vasquez and the Pentecostal Methodist Church has been warm and rewarding.

A gray haze and overcast skies lay over the city one morning—something of a contrast with the bright mornings of sunshine that had characterized these last days of summer and early days of Fall. There was a nip in the air, and John and Edna prayed that it wouldn't turn too cold yet.

When the Parkers arrived in Chile two years previously, they had felt that such sunshine also characterized their ministry in Chile, but with the passing of time, John did not think they would be staying for a long time. Along the way, he reached a place where he did not feel that he was personally needed as much as he had believed. So for some time he and Edna had felt that they needed to find other areas of service.

This decision did not affect in any way their feelings about the Institute. They felt it was a good and much needed part of the Chilean Pentecostal Movement. Dean Helland, who had become a Pentecostal Holiness missionary the year before, would remain in Chile and continue to work with the school at that time. (He later moved to Tulsa to teach in the Oral Roberts University.)

So the Parkers were moving again. They had sold their two little gas heaters, and now they were selling, giving away, and disposing of other things in different ways. They had been through this process so many times that it had become a familiar routine, although it was never exactly easy. John would soon be flying to Mexico City for a meeting with the Missions Board and then on to Oklahoma City where he would meet Edna.

Some people, like John and Edna Parker, are by nature givers. They are givers in the area of financial contributions, but also in the area of material goods. John had some very definite beliefs about two very different kinds of people, because although some are givers, others are constantly receivers. What are you? Maybe this message written by John that appeared in the *Advocate* will help you take another look at yourself, and decide about some changes you may want to make in the area of giving.

RECEIVERS AND GIVERS
John Parker

By nature we are receivers, not givers. Our innate selfishness is demonstrated in early childhood and shows little change as we grow older. It may manifest itself in mean and shoddy relationships, egotism, or a Scrooge-like miserliness. Under the whip of conscience, this disposition may undergo small improvements, but without divine help, self-seeking remains the motivating principle of our lives.

A Christian can never be like God unless he becomes a giver. To be transformed from a receiver to a giver, he must submit to a special creative work of the Holy Spirit. The Apostle Paul urged the Corinthians to excel in the grace of giving, just as they excelled *"in faith, in speech, in knowledge, in complete earnestness and in [their] love"* for the apostles. His use of the word grace (charis or charism) places giving on a spiritual plane along with all the other gifts of the Spirit. The grace of giving is a gift of the Spirit. It is a Spirit-created instinct or disposition within us.

Without this special and divine work in our nature, our efforts at giving are in constant conflict with our basic nature of selfishness. We spend lavishly on ourselves—jewelry, clothes, toys, food, recreation—much more, in fact, than that which is necessary. But our giving to others and to God is restrained, and calculated. We are careful not to give "too much."

This restraint is especially true in giving money. Satan tempts us with horrifying images of poverty, deprivation, and inadequate retirement if we give lavishly to God and His work. Our token giving is just enough to satisfy a prodding conscience or prying eyes.

Paul says that God loves a cheerful giver, that is, one who gives hilariously and with joyful abandon. That kind of giving is unrestrained, unmeasured, and uncalculated. It is faith-giving, which sees God as the source and resource of all material abundance. It gives worship to God and is a genuine expression of true holiness as it gives priority to the kingdom of God, convinced that all other things will be added.

Though the Spirit imparts the gift of giving, it may begin with our own initiative, or our own obedience to a divine command. Love is a fruit of the Spirit, and faith is both a fruit and a gift of the Spirit. But we are commanded to exercise both of them. As we obey the commands, the fruit and the gift are developed within us.

Likewise, there are commands and initiatives concerning the gift of giving. *"Give and it shall be given unto you..." "Excel in this grace of giving."* As we begin to do this as an act of obedience, the Holy Spirit works in the creation and development of the gift within us. We become by definition and disposition givers rather than takers. Giving becomes a basic spiritual instinct of our nature.

Tithing itself is not an expression of the grace of giving. Tithing is the law standard of the Old Testament and was exacted on pain of punishment. Many of us even today pay our tithes only because it is commanded. Rather than being done with joyful abandon, praise and delight, it is done to satisfy a sense of duty, a sense of rightness. That is not an unworthy motive in itself, but the New Testament standard goes beyond that. The lesser standard of the law is swallowed up in the greater standard of faith generosity, or hilarious giving.

The gift of giving is seen in a constant series of faith decisions based on a spiritual principle which has its counterpart in nature: "Whosoever sows sparingly will reap sparingly." Farmers know all about this principle. And so do faith givers. The quantity of the harvest is in direct proportion to the amount of seed sown. But is there not a selfish motive involved here? Are we to give more so that we can receive more?

If the process stops with the receiving, then, yes, selfishness does creep back into the heart. But the cycle must continue. I will give more so that I can receive more, so that I can give even more. The heart is motivated by the giving, not the receiving.

The gift of giving must be exercised in faith as are all gifts of the Spirit. "Each man should give what he has decided in his heart to give…" This is a faith promise between you and the Lord. Each Christian's decision is made in faith and it rests squarely upon God's faithfulness. You cannot give what you do not have. It is always your responsibility to believe God for whatever He has led you to commit yourself for; it is His responsibility to reward your faith by supplying what He has put into your heart to give.

God's Word tells us: *"You will be made rich in every way so that you can be generous on every occasion, and through us your generosity will result in thanksgiving to God."* This simply means that he who gives seed to the sower also ministers bread for his own table.

The old cliché, *"You cannot out-give God,"* is not an incentive for selfish investment, but a call for cooperation and commitment with God in the spreading of the Word and the building of the kingdom. We can be both givers and receivers, but the giving is dominant as a life-style.

(Printed in the International Pentecostal Holiness *ADVOCATE* /February 1986)

The lives of John and Edna Parker had been transformed by God's grace, and they were "givers." They gave of their time and their material resources; they gave an open door to friends and those in need; they gave words of blessing and encouragement; they gave of themselves. They literally invested themselves in others, so that the power of God in its fullness might go forth for the salvation of souls. They told the "good news" to those who in turn would tell others. They lived out the words of the Apostle Paul to his spiritual son, Timothy. What they had received from others, they would commit to those who would continue to share the message.

John and his brother Wiley stayed in contact over the years and were faithful to let each other know what was going on in their lives. After Wiley wrote John, he responded:

You received the right information concerning our leaving Chile...We will be leaving on May 31. I will fly to Mexico City where our Missions Board is meeting... Our plans are to live in Madrid, Spain and lend some support to the new church planting team that we are sending there.

Change had become a part of John and Edna's lives. They would set up house again, obtain legal papers, and get used to the traffic in Madrid! But a new challenge is exciting as you look ahead!

*Brethren, I do not count myself to have
apprehended; but one thing I do,
forgetting those things which are behind and
reaching forward to those things which are ahead,
I press toward the goal for the prize of the
upward call of God in Christ Jesus
(Philippians 3:13, 14).*

Chapter Seven
To Europe and the Middle East

The Parkers were to live in Madrid, but there were a series of holdups, detours, and by-paths along the way. First they were held in the States for conventions and then taking time for eye surgery. After this they were scheduled for two and one-half months in London at CICM (Centre of International Christian Ministries). Leaders would be there for those sessions from different third world countries.

John and Edna reached London in spite of the delays. During that time Jim Eby, the pastor and director of the Centre, made his apartment available to them while they were in London. It was a ten minute walk through a nice park to the Centre where they had their school activities.

They were planting a church that meets just down the street from the Centre in a primary school. About one hundred people attend every Sunday night, and most of them have been dug out of sin on the streets. This area is one of low income people, with many different races and nationalities and lots of people who are down and out. There is a high level of drug addiction, prostitution, and all that goes with those conditions. But God loves them.

The congregation is divided into four house groups that meet once a week with a leader for Bible study and prayer. One leader is British, another is from Ghana, and still another is from Ireland. John was there to serve as interim pastor until Jim Eby returned. He was also to oversee three congregations in London which were under the pastorates of Don Thomas, Nettie Storms, and Siv Mudaly. Rev. Mudaly also serves as Dean of the Centre.

The third world school began on January 16th, 1989 with a smaller number this year than in previous years. There were two from the Philippines, one from Indonesia, two from South India, one from Kenya, and one from Tanzania. Nearly all of these are pastors or leaders in their countries, and John would be teaching them for two weeks.

John was finding himself often in other countries. He flew to Cologne, West Germany to spend a couple of days with the missionaries as they were making some adjustments in the placement of personnel. All of them were deep in language study and one at least, was beginning to preach in German. John appointed him pastor of the group they are putting together which they hope will become a growing church.

From Germany, John flew over to Paris and was met by Dan Lussi who was the missionary working with our Paris church. On Sunday morning, John attended the church in Paris, about a 15 minute walk from Dan's place. It was off the street, back through an open patio kind of space, and into an old building that must have been used as a storage place or warehouse. This building had been patched up a bit, but still needed more attention. But the beauty of the place was in the people. Again, this was a mixed congregation, seemingly of every tribe, tongue, and nation. It is really a living parable of what the Church is as described in the book of the *Revelation.*

John talked with a young lady from Peru, and to another who is from Egypt who will soon graduate in pediatrics. Others were from Algiers, Ghana, the Cameroons, Greece, and who knows from where else. The worship was deeply sincere as well as joyful and reflected a high level of Christian growth and maturity. The attendance was something over a hundred though there were probably about 70 who would be considered active and committed members. About 25 of these form groups of evangelism outreach and go out on the streets every week to preach. Many individuals were brought in from the streets week by week. The goal of this one church is to start twenty new churches throughout the city of Paris. I believe they can do it!

The time spent in London was fruitful. Ten people were saved in January in the Finsbry Park Fellowship, and nine students had arrived from other countries to study urban evangelism at CICM (our centre of evangelism). Eight full-time and 13 part-time students are now studying at the London College of Christian Ministries.

John and Edna had been living out of suitcases for eight months, but their goal was always to reach Spain and be in their own place again. That goal was finally reached, and when they reached Madrid it was good to unpack again! Here they lived on the 7th floor of a ten-story apartment building right on the edge of the city. Looking out of their window, they could see an empty expanse of five miles where sheep graze, and on the distant horizon they could just make out the hangars and run-ways of the U.S. Air Force Base. Their place was a real doll house-- small that is! John said it helped them keep close together!

Since John and Edna's assignment in Spain was for Europe and the Middle East, John asked the question, *Is Europe a mission field?* Although the question can be argued and debated, it can't be ignored. In her religious history, Europe counts such evangelical stalwarts as Luther, Knox, Wesley, and Spurgeon. North America received her Protestant beginnings from Europe. But how was Europe when John took over his job? Take a look at these 1989 statistics when John was taking up residence there! At that time...

- Only 20% of all Europeans were Protestants and barely two percent of them were truly born-again.
- Only 1% of the French people were Protestants, and most of them were not saved.
- In England more Muslims worshipped on Friday than Anglicans who worshipped on Sunday.
- Only 7% of all Europeans ever attend church.
- There were 250,000 cities and towns in Europe that did not have an Evangelical Church.

Is Europe a mission field? What do you think?

Edna spent five weeks in her new apartment, and then on May 1 she went back to North Carolina to care for her sick mother. There was no one else to do that, and Edna responded to that need. John, however found this time of absence difficult. After a six-week five-nation tour of Europe and the Middle East which took him from Spain to Israel, Egypt, Italy, and England, he was really missing Edna, and he wrote in a newsletter:

Separation is not easy for a couple that has loved each other for forty years. We will return to Spain and fields of labor just after Christmas. Between now and then, I will do a three-week study course at Columbia Bible College in South Carolina.

It was May of 1989, and as John and Edna analyzed their future, they considered that the work ahead of them in Eastern Europe would be a great challenge. Don and Rose Gentilini had just been appointed as our first missionaries to Eastern Europe. A Mug-a-Month Coffee House had been opened in Budapest, Hungary, and each Wednesday night about 120 young people, many of them drug addicts, alcoholics, gang leaders, and street people, crowd the premises to hear the Word. What a tremendous challenge!

John asked himself the question as to how a person could live in two worlds at the same time. Well, he observed that they had actually done that for several months. Edna was with her mother, and John was involved in the U.S.: General Conference, the School of Missions, and a number of other special meetings.

But finally John and Edna were back together in Spain. Here they were usually in several meetings each week to encourage and support the different groups in Madrid. They personally had a group in Madrid, and they met with them two or three times a week when they were in the city.

The Parkers were people with a global world view. They always took advantage of their visits to the different nations to know the people and the world they lived in. They wanted to know about their industries, where they worked, what they ate, and the natural world in which they lived.

At one time John and Edna had the opportunity to go with Supervisor Lin Berry and his family on a tour of Spain. The trip from Madrid led them through a fantastic landscape of olive groves and vineyards. Most of it was Don Quijote country that was complete with windmills and everything else. The area is called La Mancha, and the special cheese made in the area comes from sheep milk and is called Manchego cheese.

On the coast they saw vast groves of oranges and lemons. Vineyards dotted the landscapes in some areas, and the trees in the olive groves were lined up across the mountains and in the valleys. While there they discovered the Valencia oranges which are now famous around the world. The Parkers had eaten oranges from many different parts of the world, but none could touch the sweetness of the Spanish oranges. Their tour also included a trip down the Mediterranean coast just to see the marvelous world of God's creation.

Not only were they interested in Spain, however, but in addition to their residence there, they maintained contact with seven other areas of ministry which the church had in Europe and the Middle East. John wrote…

Stubborn resistance is being met from the enemy all over Europe, but the concentrated firepower of prayer and fasting is bringing a lot of pressure on him. The devil is weak in direct proportion to the praying of the Church. People, let's pray!

And God was at work! The doors into Eastern Europe began to open! In November of 1989 the people of East Germany were given freedom to go into West Germany, and then the Berlin wall was broken down! Dramatic, unbelievable and mind-boggling events were taking place in Europe during that time! Only God could have battered down the atheistic, communistic and iron-fisted oppression that those countries labored under! Why did God do it? He did it to open a window of opportunity for the preaching of the Gospel!

Don Gentilini, our missionary living near Vienna, just a short time after the opening came, went into Romania on three different occasions. On the third opportunity, he and others took in 1,500 Bibles for distribution along with $50,000 of donated medical supplies. His team preached eleven times in eight days and saw Romanian Christians baptized in the Holy Spirit in each service. The country was filled with an unbelievable hunger and thirst for the Living Word and for the Living God.

A Summer Action Team led by Don Gentilini did 80 hours of teaching to 100 pastors and Christian leaders in July. In four nights of evangelistic preaching, between 500 and 600 people received Jesus as Lord of their lives. Romania, the most oppressed country in Eastern Europe, was experiencing revival!

The leaders quickly began to set up some new goals. They needed to place in Budapest a missionary who could plant an international congregation in English and who would also set up a Pentecostal Holiness training school in Eastern Europe.

On to Rome! A Bible training school that began in October had ten students enrolled for the first class to study the book of Acts. The Coffee House activities had increased as well as those in the Piazza Navona. Elders and ministers were meeting regularly to prepare for leadership roles. John reported that four house groups met each week and combined their worship on Sunday evenings. This was the result of intense prayer and work in this city.

Evangelism forays continued on down to Naples. Two open-air services in the Dante Plaza in Naples were bringing a response. Each nation touched John's heart profoundly, and his cry was: Pray for a church to be planted in the near future in Naples!

From France! Dan Lussi reported that the Living Rock Church in Paris was continuing to reach out in apostolic witness on the streets of the city. There were very few born-again Christians in the country, but greater is He that is within us than he that is in the world!

The enemy is desperately trying to hold on to France. A young Algerian, who was saved in Paris, returned to his own country, and he soon received two death threats from Muslim extremists. He was in hiding until safe passage could be assured for him to leave his country. Many have been bound by satanic oppression and superstition, but the power of God is all sufficient and able to deliver!

Sometimes John's visits were just to encourage the leaders and see how the work was moving forward. His assessment was that the German work was tough and that the principle work of our missionaries at this time was to learn the language, get to know the people, and to win their confidence. The German people do not readily commit themselves to us and our church unless they are absolutely sure that we are there to stay. They are careful to align themselves only with a group that is trustworthy and credible.

Our coffee house there was open and running, and a number of people had dropped in just to check us out, but some had returned. Only God can move these people and cause them to experience genuine conversion. John preached in the service on Sunday night—the first time he had preached in Germany! At this time he had preached in about 28 different countries, and he would continue to reach out and minister in other nations of the global!

During this time John and Edna also went to Egypt and were joined by Brothers Simmons and Goodson. The four of them had a good seminar with the pastors and churches in Assiut, which is about 200 miles south of Cairo. They preached in four different churches at night, and all of them were packed to capacity. There was still quite a bit of opposition from the Muslims, and there are always risks to be taken with the gospel.

Taking such a risk is one of the prices of being a Christian, and such a risk was taken by Missionary William Robinson. He was shot by Muslim extremists in southern Lebanon the same week John and Edna were in Egypt.

At the end of 1990, John wrote:

> *The year 1990 has been a good year for the Kingdom of God, for the Pentecostal Holiness Church, and for our witness and work in Europe and the Middle East. We have seen advance and victory in each place where our missionaries are working. Missionaries have gone into Budapest; more people have been saved in London; the Living Rock church in Paris is stabilized and strengthened. Rome, Madrid, and our coffee house in Germany are showing marked victories, the EERC (Eastern European Resource Center) project in Hungary is well on the way to realization, and missionaries have gone into the USSR!*

John and Edna were blessed as they continued to receive answers to prayer.

- Thirteen excellent students were enrolled in the International School of Urban Ministries as Jim and Peggy Eby continued to give inspired leadership in London.

- There was now a church in Rome! An English speaking congregation, the Casal Palocco Evangelical Church had joined hands and heart with us to reach the lost. This historic center church is located in the heart of ancient Rome, and by that time they had reached 40 in attendance and had set a goal of 100 this year.

- In Spain the open air crusades held last summer in Madrid had greatly increased their contacts and outreach. The Berry's living room was full on Tuesday evenings and spiritual excitement was at a high pitch as the Lord applied the Word to the hearts of the people.

- In Hungary, Dan and Rose Gentilini were living in the Eastern European Resource Centre (EERC) and were working to furnish and equip it for classes which were to begin on April 1. They were also working hard studying the Hungarian language.

- In the Soviet Union George and Theresa Sherry were at work in the Ukraine. In four months, George reported that he...

  * had shown the JESUS film to 10,000 people.
  * had preached in fifteen different cities.
  * was working with public school authorities for permission to teach the Bible to students.
  * was preparing to plant a church in Rovno

- Moscow has become a "hot spot" of mass response to the gospel. Many are clamoring to hear "more about Jesus." Two couples are being assigned to go there for the purpose of opening more churches.

- Romania is still wide open to the gospel and plans are on foot to open a training school next year.
- Albania, long declared to be an atheist nation, now welcomes Christian ministry.

It is hard to imagine two weeks packed with more dramatic events than those the Parkers were witnessing at this time. A coup by hard-line communists in the Soviet Union was crushed by the will of the people. Gorbachev, the USSR President, resigned from the Communist Party and recommended that the Party be dismantled. Ten republics of the USSR passed motions of independence. The Baltic States, Lithuania, Estonia, and Latvia were set free. Power was shifted from Moscow to the remaining USSR republics.

John could only ask himself if this was all going to lead to chaos, confusion, and even more danger, or if it was a mighty wind of freedom blowing across the land. One thing was certain! The doors were wide open for the preaching of the gospel and our missionaries, George and Theresa Sherry, were taking full advantage of it. They seemed ready even then to purchase a building that would serve as a missionary home, office, and evangelism outreach center in Rovno.

As of August 7, our Pentecostal Holiness Church received full registration in Russia as a religious body with full legal and statutory rights. Our first church in the city of Rovno now numbers about 100 people. God is indeed at work!

On a visit to the island of Malta, located off the coast of Sicily, John found himself on St. Paul's Bay, the traditional site of the Apostle Paul's shipwreck. With the dark blue waters crashing on the rocks and a strong wind blowing in his face, it was easy to recreate in his mind the scene of Paul's arrival.

For fourteen days and nights, the storm-tossed passengers had seen neither sun nor stars. Despairing of life, the sailors ceased any effort to save the ship, leaving it and themselves to the mercy of wind and waves. Then Paul, the great Apostle, stood forth declaring that God had spoken to him, and that no one would be lost. They were to be of good cheer and eat some food. On this fourteenth day, the ship crashed upon the rocks of Malta and split apart, but just as Paul had said, all lives were saved.

But John Parker had not come through storm and shipwreck that day. He had come through bright sunshine to receive a warm Christian welcome from Pastor Joe Agius. Brother Agius is a native of Malta who had opened a Pentecostal Holiness Church in that island nation. Now Pastor Agius and the Christians who made up the churches were there with extended hands and smiles on their faces. John had come to offer them encouragement and counsel, to teach the scriptures, and to assure these dear people that though they were living on a small island in the middle of the Mediterranean, they were objects of God's love and grace.

During his stay, John preached five times, ordained an elder and a deacon, visited several homes, and gave encouragement to the pastor and his people. The work in Malta now consisted of three different groups, one on each of the two islands and a group of 15-20 inmates who had been won to the Lord in the local prison. John was pleased to learn that Pastor Agius was planning on continuing his ministerial preparation by becoming a student in our school in London.

John's life was a busy round of activities in different nations. John and Edna made a trip to Costa Rica where John taught Advanced Ministerial Training classes. The highlight of their trip was a visit to the jungle area of Sarapiqui, but they didn't see the little green and white church that John had built in 1963. It was nowhere in sight, and neither was the little rustic house across the street which had served as their first preaching point in 1955. They did find, however, a fine new concrete church building twice the size of the first one. This one had been financed entirely by the local congregation! To God be the glory for the great things He had done in this beautiful country where they had labored for twenty-three happy years.

The following month, John participated in a graduation service for twenty students of CICM in London. Over 200 attended the program and their shouts of praise and worship accompanied every activity of the service.

Then there was the great missionary retreat they had in the lovely surroundings of Switzerland! It was so special that Edna could be with him. It was a time of blessing, rest and fellowship as they met together for days of prayer, worship and study. They went deep into the biblical solutions to problems of fear, low self-esteem, forgiveness, and personal relationships. John counted it a privilege to minister to the missionary families who worked in different areas of Europe.

In September, John spent a week in Moscow teaching Basic Doctrines at the Agape Training Center. The sixty students had come from Russia, Kazahkstan, Uzbekistan, and the Caucases. These are the people whom God is raising up as leaders for churches being planted all across the former Soviet

Union. While there John consulted our personnel in Moscow to discuss strategies for turning house groups into organized churches.

Leaving Moscow, John flew to Kiev, Ukraine where he was met by George Sherry and Brother Sasha. The next day (Sunday), he worshipped with the fine congregation which George and Theresa had planted in the three years they had served in the Ukraine. There were over 100 in attendance and worship was lifted to God in spirit and in truth. They ordained Brother Sasha as an interim pastor and received 43 people as new members.

Riding eastward toward Kiev in the early morning darkness to meet his departure schedule, John watched a rosy dawn brighten as the sun's red ball exploded into bright light over the flat Ukranian plain. He gave God the glory for the spiritual light that was spreading the gospel across those same plains. Surely the Holy Spirit with power was moving into the towns, villages, and farm hamlets to bring salvation and blessing to the hungry people who were living there.

John's last trip to Europe included a stopover in Spain where he inspected the new church-planting institute. Located in a building over one hundred years old, it stood on the Plaza Santo Domingo in the very heart of Madrid with some 20 rooms. It would provide a dormitory, classrooms, dining area, and sanitary facilities.

John also ministered in the two churches we had in Spain at that time: on Sunday morning to the people in Madrid and on Sunday evening to those in in Parla. Then on Saturday there were twenty Spirit-filled people who met all day for leadership training. John enjoyed preaching and ministering to these people in their churches, but it was the sessions in leadership training that gave him the greatest sense of fulfillment.

But change was coming. For the past seven years John and Edna had been sending newsletters about their work as Supervisors of Europe and the Middle East. During that time, they had told about the expanding work in Western Europe in countries such as England, France, Spain, Italy and Germany. He had informed his readers of the affiliation of ten churches in Egypt with the Pentecostal Holiness Church. They had also been able to follow the coffee house ministries, the ministries in the houses and the assignment of missionaries to the unreached peoples of North Africa.

The most dramatic development in that part of the world during this time, of course, had been the liberation of the Eastern European countries and the breakup of the Soviet Union. Suddenly these countries were no longer closed to the Gospel. Ministers, missionaries and Christians could go in, take Bibles, minister the Word and start new churches.

To be able to move into those nations where we had previously been unable to take the message of the cross, was not only a blessing, but also a great challenge! We soon learned that the people were very hungry for God and anxious to hear and study His Word. Soon believers who had stood true to their witness through the years could go "public" and become a part of our work. New churches sprang up as souls were saved and delivered. John and Edna were indeed thankful for the ministry of the church. It was a great blessing to see new missionaries become a part of God's work and the expansion of His kingdom in that part of the world!

John wrote…

The work of supervising the outreach of the Pentecostal Holiness Church in Europe and the Middle East is in some respects the most exciting and challenging of all that we have done over the last forty years… It is good that we did not know exactly all that we would face… All we did know was that God had laid His hand upon us and called us out to go.

You responded in obedience to the same Lord and over these many years, you have stood behind us with your support, concern, and prayers. Together, you have made a difference with us in the lives of many precious souls who will in that day rise up and call us "blessed."

So John and Edna would soon be saying "goodbye" as Supervisors in this part of the world. But they had followed the Lord for many years and experienced many changes. They had learned to trust God and to be led by those who directed the worldwide program of missions through the church.

It seemed to them that they had never had to worry about how they would make ends meet. God always supplied the finances they needed through the faithfulness of their supporters. When they finished one assignment, there was always another assignment waiting for them. And there had always been faithful people ready to support them in their work.

By this time they had lived on four different continents and ministered in 35 countries over a period of 42 years of missionary labor. And yes, there was a new assignment waiting for them. As God had directed their paths in the past, He would continue to direct them wherever they would go in the future.

The Holy Spirit is there; He always keeps God's children in His path.

> *However, when He,*
> *the Spirit of truth, has come,*
> *He will guide you into all truth*
> (John 16:13).

Chapter Eight
Roving Missionary Teacher

John and Edna again faced a new challenge. Their new responsibility was an assignment recently made by the administrative staff of the World Missions Department. The staff asked John to become a Special Assignment Instructor for Christian Education. This was a full-time position that would require John and Edna to go anywhere in the world where the church had schools and training centers. John said that the position seemed to be a divinely-ordered finish to all that they had done and would do to build the Kingdom of Christ around the world.

John and Edna were continually expressing their appreciation to those who supported them in their missionary work. In writing to those involved, He said it as follows in his own words:

None of this would have been possible without your participation and burden for the unreached and lost people of the world. We could not have gone without you. Your strong prayers and faithful giving are your obedience to the cry of God's

*own heart and the command of Christ our Lord.
We continue to need those strong prayers and the
faithful giving.*

John had teaching trips planned in 1994 for Singapore, Venezuela, Trinidad, Mexico City, London,
and Argentina. Other requests for his help were
forthcoming. This would demand hours and days of
study and preparation, days of travel under varied
conditions, and hundreds of hours in the classroom.
Again John called on his partners in the faith to pray
for him in this new venture:

*Pray that our ministry of teaching and preaching
(and our conversations) will be anointed with
heaven's wisdom as well as with heaven's fire.
Nothing is more deadening than preaching without passion or teaching without authority*

On the way to Singapore, John declared that the
Pacific Ocean seemed much wider than it had been
on his last crossing in 1987. He was absolutely sure
that there had been severe erosion on both sides!

His class in Singapore was a mixture of students
from different countries: Malaysia, the Philippines,
and Indonesia. These students were already deeply
involved in ministry responsibilities. Together they
would pursue an in-depth study of the book of Ro-

mans that would help them understand the "Righteousness of God."

John's return from Singapore took him to Hong Kong where he visited missionaries and renewed old acquaintances. The growth of the work in the seven years they had been gone was very encouraging. John continued his teaching tour in Venezuela then on to Trinidad. There was a severe water shortage in Venezuela, but he told Edna that they were getting enough to stay decent! He was teaching *Holiness-Pentecostal History* and *Contemporary Theological Issues* – and all in his favorite second language (Spanish)!

When John left on this trip, he left Edna with her "to do" list which at the last moment included the preparation of the next newsletter. She felt it was time to "brag" a bit about their family, so she took advantage of the opportunity to include news about the children.

A missionary's family is vital to him and his wife. At times children rebel and do not always respond to the many changes that are involved in the life of a missionary. John and Edna did not experience this, however, with their son, David. At the time of this writing he was living in Oklahoma City and employed as a project manager in data processing. His wife, Irvina, was working in the

World Missions Department of the church and did a lot of work in the area of publishing and promotion. As to the grandchildren, Ryan, was just four months away from being a teenager and a very good student. Jennifer, in the fourth grade would soon be ten years old and made good grades. She was recently baptized in water and joined the church. This was what really made the heart of grandparents rejoice! They had grown up so quickly!

At this point in time it was Edna's job to keep the home fires burning while she cared for her 88-year old mother. In addition she worked growing flowers and vegetables in the garden—especially the tomatoes that John loved so much. Whether she was at home or abroad, however, Edna's heart was bound to that of her husband and to the work God had called him to do.

According to Matthew 4:23, the ministry of Jesus was done within three well-defined dimensions: those of teaching, preaching, and healing. The people addressed Jesus as Rabbi, which was the title given to a teacher in ancient Judaism. In Matthew 7:28, it is written that the people were amazed at his teaching for He taught them as one having authority and not as their scribes.

A vital part of the Great Commission in Matthew 28:16-20 is that the apostles and followers of Jesus were to teach the nations all the things that He had taught them. Though powerful and anointed preaching is necessary to build the church and establish conviction concerning divine truth, the church will ultimately stand or fall on the quality of teaching it receives.

So important is teaching in the church that the Holy Spirit has linked teaching as a companion gift to the ministry gift of pastoring (Ephesians 4:11). John had known for years that teaching was one of his strongest gifts, and he felt a deep and satisfying joy in teaching the Word of God to those who yearned for the truth.

Recently he had taught twenty-four students at CICM in London. Together they had delved into a study of World Religions and Cults. Really it is not a very edifying study, but it is certainly important as well as instructive. There were moments in class when praise and worship erupted among the students as they contrasted the wonderful salvation they had as a gift from God to the fearful desperation of millions caught in the devil's trap of delusion.

What a blessing to be a blessing! The students were expressive in making their comments about the class and were grateful for the insight they had received. Here are some of the responses of the students to the teaching they received:

- Mauricio Salazar (Mexico)

  It was a very helpful class. I was especially surprised at some of the teachings that I did not know. I praise God for saving me from the dangers of these terrible religious heresies.

- Olivia Nikkanen (Finland)

  It is very important that we know about these cults and what they teach, for we have to face them daily. We must know how to respond to those who are attached to them. Thank you for the materials you have given to us. Very useful!

- Austen Egierbor (Nigeria)

  The course was a blessing to me, especially the information about the New Age Movement. The resource materials given to us are great... Thanks!

- Carmen Banks (Philippines)

  This study gives me a firmer faith in my salvation. Thanks to Mr. Parker for giving us information helpful in witnessing to these nonbelievers who need to know the truth.

- Paul B Akinwale (Nigeria)

  For the first time in my life I have been exposed to the Eastern religions. I intend to increase my studies in these areas and alert my church concerning these dangerous cults.

- Bernard P Ankomah (Ghana)
  Enlightened by this study, I have a deeper burden to reach those attached to cults... Many of them were built upon errors in the interpretation of the Scriptures.

- George Sempa (Uganda)
  The study not only gives understanding as to what false religions believe and teach, but it also shows us how we can reach them for Christ. Thank you so much for making these materials available.

John's next trip was to Caracas, Venezuela. He had been there on numerous occasions, but he was always fascinated by this megacity. It stretches along the floor of a narrow valley about 15 miles long and approximately two miles wide. Compressed between the mountain ranges, it was an assortment of industry, commerce and residential dwellings all ranging from 1 to 25 floors. That in itself was not striking, for the same could be said of many cities in the world.

What was different about Caracas was that it was full of large American cars, some of them new but most of them old. One marveled at the skill of the home-grown mechanics who kept these fuel-hungry monsters running, and he wondered, *Why are there so many of them?* Astoundingly, gasoline was only 10 to 15 cents per gallon! He learned that the government heavily subsidized the price of fuel so that the people could feel that they were enjoying a share of the country's wealth.

He remembered also that this was the country where Charlene West ministered after leaving Costa Rica. She had helped build the work on a solid foundation, and it had continued to grow with Missionaries Gary and Kathy (West) Petty and the national leadership. In the past John had taught there while Charlene was supervising the work in Venezuela and Colombia.

During John's visit in September of 1994, a revival broke out in the town of Ocumare, two hours from Caracas. On a Sunday night, 50 rejoicing Christians were filled with the Holy Spirit according to Acts 2. The meeting lasted until 1:00 A.M. and the streets were filled with wondering neighbors. Could this be the spiritual breeze of God that they were praying for? Was the power of the Spirit getting ready to sweep over this nation? Oh, we trust that the Holy Spirit will visit these people from the Caribbean coast to deep into the rain-forest and from the oil-splattered surface of Lake Maracaibo to the mighty Orinoco River.

John's students were receptive to his teaching, and wrote their expressions of appreciation. The Conference Superintendent and pastor of the mother church in Caracas,

Hernando Brochero wrote:

> *Your study on False Cults is a positive contribution to maintaining our true Christian faith. It is an antidote against the spiritual sickness that would damage the divine revelation that God has given us.*

Juan Octavio Sierra wrote:

> *Your teachings on the Sixteen Principles of New Testament Evangelism have made a great impression on my own life and ministry. I will endeavor to put them into practice in my ministry.*

As in Venezuela, so it was in Argentina. His students responded with beautiful and rewarding expressions of their appreciation to God and to their teacher. Here are some of the expressions they took time to turn in. Julio wrote:

> *The study of the Book of Romans has been a great intellectual and spiritual blessing. It has*

given me a clearer understanding of what salvation really is and how it comes to us.

Hugo said:

The study of Romans really put my understanding of this great epistle in order and helped me see what is important to God. It also greatly enhanced my estimation of the Apostle Paul and his ministry. He is worthy to be imitated.

Back in the U.S. again, John was now about to cross the Pacific Ocean from Raleigh, North Carolina. In the past twenty years, he had crossed it 35 times, and one would think that with so many flights, he would get accustomed to it. He didn't think so! When he boarded the plane to make the crossing this time, he did so with a fever, a tight chest, congestion, and a deep cough. He was suffering with whatever half of his town's inhabitants had come down with! He arrived in Manila about 11:30 P.M., and got four hours of sleep to be up again for a five hour drive to Baguio City. They would begin this seminar with the pastors and workers of the churches in the Philippians.

After struggling through the first three hours, John sought some way to get a penicillin shot to clear out his fever. The only doctor that Missionary Debra Crook knew was a lady gynecologist, so to her they went. He had no idea what the crowd of women waiting in her office thought when he walked in, but he was soon behind closed doors getting the desired treatment. By depending on the Lord, the One who is really our Healer, John got the shot, and the job got done!

From Manila, John headed for Madras, India. He ended up seated in row number 63 at the very end of the plane. It also put him at the end of a very long line of passengers going through immigration. Something happened that night that had never happened before: He was absolutely the last person out of 400 that went through immigration that night! Brother Vidyasagar was waiting for him like the very attentive host that he had always been in the past.

John then flew on to Hyderabad where he had visited nine years before when Brother Kumar was just beginning his church planting efforts. In the intervening years four congregations had begun, and a fine church building as well as the Kenneth Donald training facility had been constructed. About 25 students were enrolled and divided into two classes, and they had a wonderful week of fellowship, teaching and learning. Brother Kew Sun was John's teaching partner, and they teased each other about their strengths and weaknesses. John cautioned him about not speaking English too fast, and he in turn, chided John for using too many big words!

But there were changes in the country. Coca Cola and Pepsi were now in, and they were quenching many thirsty throats, and more important, John could send a FAX to Edna from his hotel! The traffic was the same or worse. Every describable kind of vehicle along with the cows, goats, and at least one monkey were all fighting for space. There must have been at least ten thousand incidents where a tragedy was averted by only half an inch. But how wonderful is the grace of God for both saint and sinner! John witnessed only one collision in an entire week—a light bump between a motor scooter and a pushcart!

John's next teaching assignment was a wonderful week in Mexicali teaching the book of Romans and a course on Sanctification to 35 students. The latter study was requested by the people themselves, and they threw themselves into it with great enthusiasm. The work in West Mexico was moving forward. In Mexicali alone, the conference now had ten churches and 1,800 members. The pastors had a great vision for expansion as they looked forward to the future.

In the midst of the busy times of travel and ministry, John and Edna experienced the sadness of family loss. On April 18, Edna's brother-in-law, Tryon

Lowry, died of a sudden heart attack. He was about 50 years old and within the past two years had just completed his studies at Duke University while pastoring two Methodist churches in Rockingham, North Carolina. His funeral was conducted at the Pentecostal Holiness Church in Pembroke, North Carolina with 700 people present, including about 50 Methodist ministers!

Then on July 24, Edna's mother passed away at the age of 89 after several years of declining health. Her death came ten days after a heavy stroke which left her unconscious and unable to eat or drink. Her funeral was a simple one which took place in the Pentecostal Holiness Church of Garland, North Carolina. She was laid to rest beside her husband who had passed away in 1946.

Edna's mother's death caused a major readjustment in the Parker's lives. During the previous five years, Edna had cared for her mother, while John had traveled alone. She hadn't been able to accompany him very much, but they did not regret the years of caring, even though it had restricted them in many ways. Filial duty is a strong biblical teaching, and even during the years of their overseas residence in missions work John and Edna had tried to be as attentive as possible to her mother's needs.

When these things take place changes are necessary, but time moves on, and the future must be faced. The next stop was in London at CICM, and John taught the *History and Principles of Revival*. Most of the 25 students were African Christians, and John loved their singing. He asked them to sing a couple of times, for in his opinion there was no singing in the world that was so moving as African singing. It comes out in deep melodious harmonies that swell and reach out to envelop the soul and spirit. It almost sounds as if every musical note of the universe has come together in praise and adoration to the Creator. What a blessing!

John arrived at his next appointment in Costa Rica at a time when the entire country was blanketed with a heavy threatening thunderhead that was reaching high into the sky. He wasn't afraid, but perhaps just a little concerned. This is rugged and mountainous country with tricky winds that have actually torn planes apart. Several aircraft with all their crew and passengers have disappeared either into the ocean or thick jungle growth and have never been found. However, the skill of our pilots, the expertise of those in the control tower, and our good guardian Lord brought us down safely. It was great to be back in Costa Rica.

The following day John began teaching *Romans* and *Pastoral Psychology*. Their total enrollment was 62—the highest enrollment of any Advanced Teaching Course (CURSUM) since the program began.

In August it was on to Caracas, Venezuela for John to teach *Spiritual Warfare* and *Missiology*. This was a study focused primarily on cross-cultural communication. These mission fields had been blessed by receiving from missionaries who had come to them from other cultures, but this study challenged them to cross cultural ministry themselves. They would have to break the barriers!

It was after this time that John, Edna, David, Irvina and their family took time out for a Costa Rican family vacation. They visited some places familiar to them and others that were not. Among the latter was the Volcano Arenal, an active and thundering monster at whose base they spent one night (which happened to be John's birthday!). They were surrounded by thick rain forest, the roar of frequent explosions, the fussing and fuming of howler monkeys, and the raucous call of jungle birds flitting back and forth. Since they were less than a mile from the crater, they had a grandstand view!

Later it was early in October 1995, and the year was slipping away. According to John's schedule, however, he was to teach in five more countries before the end of the year: India, Indonesia, Costa Rica, Spain and England. This would involve thousands of miles of flying, several nights with little or no sleep, and abrupt changes in time, schedules, food, weather and cultures. But a missionary's life is full of changes. The missionary has to be mobile, ready to move, ready to fight, and always ready for the unexpected.

And the unexpected came when he got a report back after his physical exam. His doctor called saying *Mr. Parker, we have a problem. Your recent biopsy reveals that you have a malignancy in the prostate gland.* John quickly rejected the urge to panic as he conversed with his doctor about the situation. They ended up by scheduling surgery for October 31. That would leave him time to make his scheduled trip to India and Indonesia, but he would have to cancel trips to Costa Rica, the School of Missions in Oklahoma City, and a trip to Spain. He left the visit to London on schedule since his doctor felt that his recuperation would come along fast enough to permit that.

John's trip to the Far East (India) proved to be a difficult one. Hurricane Opal had slammed into the Gulf Coast the night before and every plane schedule on the east coast was disrupted. Serious winds caused an hour's delay in his departure from Raleigh, North Carolina, and in Atlanta he missed his connecting flight by two minutes. He had to reschedule in San Francisco ten hours late for Singapore getting just three hours sleep in a day room at the airport. He left for Madras, India on schedule and got four hours of sleep in a nondescript hotel there. His flight for Hyderabad the next morning was delayed by six hours because of engine trouble. He arrived at 4:30 in the afternoon, went directly to his hotel, had a quick cup of tea, and tumbled into bed for 10 hours of sleep—non-stop. Since leaving home, he had endured 26 hours of flight time and 32 of waiting time. Oh, the joys of travel!

The beautiful week with the students, however, was great. He had ten students, and they plunged into the book of *Romans* with him. According to Professor John nearly every major study topic in the Bible is dealt with in this one epistle, especially those having to do with God's way of salvation. Their five days went altogether too quick.

John left Hyderabad on Friday night, and jostled his way among 400 passengers headed for Singapore. He arrived at 7:00 in the morning just in time to get his flight to Medan, Indonesia. The pastor was a brother John had taught in London several years before. The next day, he worshipped with a joyful congregation that was made up mostly of new Christians. The service was special. He had vividly remembered the ardent worship and beautiful singing of the Indonesian people from a previous trip.

John's teaching was sandwiched among singing, worship, prayer, testimonies, and breaks for refreshments of coffee, tea, fruit juices and Indonesian hors d'oeuvres. Again he taught the book of *Romans*, because he felt that his intended subject, *Contemporary Theological Issues*, would be a bit out of place. His students turned out to be the whole church with ages from 15 to 75!

John could see great possibilities for God's work under the leadership of these people. Medan is a growing city, literally vibrating with new businesses, hotels, and accommodations for tourists. It was just the kind of place where a growing church could make a mark for the Kingdom of God. He believed that these Indonesian Christians would be able to do just that.

But it was home again, and he had a surgery to face. John and Edna had gotten complete victory through prayer, and they felt that everything would be fine. The surgery, as scheduled, took place on October 31, and John got along remarkably well. It was the first time he had ever spent a night in a hospital! According to the physician, all was contained in the prostate gland; within six months, however, it could have spread to other parts of his body. How they thanked the Lord for an early diagnosis!

His doctor released him to go home after five days for four weeks of recuperation. People had been remembering him and prayers had been going up in his behalf. He was overcome by the flood of letters, cards, flowers, and visits. When he talked to David about this, his son laconically said, *Well, Dad, you've been around a long time.*

John's recovery was rapid, and in a short month, he was off again to London for another teaching assignment the first week in December! John taught a course there on Luke's *Theology of the Holy Spirit.*

But now Christmas time was coming around again, and John and Edna would be with their family in Oklahoma City. David and Irvina, along with the grandchildren Ryan and Jennifer, were expecting them for the holidays. They were so blessed to see the spiritual growth of Ryan and Jennifer and noticed that they even called the family's attention to the daily devotional time and then took a lead in it! This was truly something for John and Edna to rejoice about.

After Christmas, John and Edna flew on down to Monterrey, Mexico and stayed with Judy and Ruben Perez for a couple of weeks. John taught in the advanced seminar (CURSUM) and then spent five days with a group of 15 Bible Institute students who were going through the basic elements of biblical salvation. He was greatly impressed by their punctuality in class and their maturity in asking questions.

John kept a daily journal throughout his ministry, and it is a challenge to walk with him through some of those notes and experience the work he did in his travels to so many different places here, there and everywhere! He tells a bit about his way of doing things in the following note:

> *I cannot say that all my travel is pleasant and enjoyable, or that the places where I stay are always comfortable. I do not ride first class or stay in five star hotels. The joy and satisfaction of my work lies in the continuing fulfillment of the divine call I received so many years ago, and the pure delight of ministering the Word of God to so many people in so many different places.*

In the 1996 commencement exercises of Southwestern College of Christian Ministries (now Southwestern Christian University) John was awarded an honorary doctorate from that institution. This honor came to him as a surprise. Later on May the first of 1996, John received a letter from Ronald Moore, the President of Southwestern, and he wrote the following words of appreciation and thanksgiving for his work and ministry:

May 1, 1996

Thank you so much for allowing us the privilege to honor you, your life and ministry on this past Sunday. You certainly epitomize to me what the honorary title of Doctor of Divinity is all about. I thank God for you and for the privilege of know-ing you and the distinguished ministry which God has accomplished through you.

> *President Ronald Moore*
> *Southwestern College of*
> *Christian Ministries*

John was blessed to be honored in this way, and also to receive letters from friends who were happy that he had been so honored. To John it exemplified to a small degree the love he had for his work.

A short time later, he received a letter from an old friend he had known for many years. Kenneth Mulholland had become the Dean and Professor of Missions and Ministry Studies at Columbia Biblical Seminary and Graduate School of Missions in Colombia, South Carolina where he had also studied. It was a joy to hear from one he had known for so many years.

John Parker

Dear John:

What a special privilege it was to read just this week about the Honorary Doctorate which Southwestern College of Christian Ministries bestowed upon you. It is well deserved!

And I'm glad to see Columbia listed among those institutions at which you studied. You enriched the very students with whom you studied in class discussions, in personal conversation, and in the "Window on the World" forum during chapel.

God has used you significantly in many ways and in many parts of the world during your long and varied ministry...May God continue to use you as a channel of blessing for His people.

Ken

Strangely enough, John did not add the doctoral title, which he so richly deserved, to his correspondence. Perhaps many people did not even realize that Southwestern College had awarded it to him. To his many friends and wide public he just continued to be known as their missionary, John B. Parker.

John went to many different areas repeatedly, yet it is interesting that in writing he always added experiences that were special at that particular place and in that precise moment.

Concordia, Argentina

The Canavesios and I stayed in the home with a dear oldie called "Doña" Menta. Her home was comfortable in an old-fashioned way: fans to keep cool, little water in the bathroom faucet but none in the shower! The defining thing about this place, however, was not the little house, but the little hostess. Doña Menta was a high quality jewel—a godly saint whose love and motives were so pure and unfeigned that to have refused her hospitality would have been a sin of the worst kind.

Villa Eliza, Paraguay

This church was started by a congregation from Buenos Aires, Argentina pastored by Enrique Coronel. This pastor made many evangelism trips as he and his people took donations in order to purchase and renovate a building previously used for storage. It was a pressing need, and they had done a great job involving their people in this missionary project. What a very beautiful and victorious time we had! Seventy-five people made up this new outreach ministry.

Mexicali, Mexico

I ministered to the Good Samaritan congregation on Sunday morning, and we all enjoyed an unusual anointing of the Holy Spirit. The musicians played some old hymns such as There is a Fountain Filled with Blood, I Love to Tell the Story and At the Cross. Wave after wave of glory and power moved across the people. They bent under it as wheat bends to the wind. A Latin American congregation touched with the glow of the Spirit is a beautiful sight to behold. To God be the glory!

Costa Rica

I was off to Costa Rica for two weeks of teaching. I arrived at midday, and I stopped on my way to the Bible Institute to visit with Pedro and Iveth Murillo. They had recently retired after having served 40 years in a ministry I helped them launch in the early fifties! Later Edna and I attended the 50th anniversary of the founding of our work in Costa Rica.

London (CICM)

Most of the students on this trip were Africans, some living in London and others coming from their own countries of Ghana, Nigeria, Kenya, and Malawi. Among them was the former director of a Bible college in Ghana and also a bishop from a large group of churches in Nigeria. In the study on revival, I showed the class a video from Promise Keepers [that had to do with a service for racial reconciliation] ...

Clergy Conference of Promise Keepers

Some students wept as they witnessed the awesome scenes of reconciliation that occurred among 40,000 clergy – black and white and other racially divided groups. A Japanese brother begged forgiveness of the Chinese and other Orientals for the cruelties perpetrated by his nation during World War II. All this affected the class, since most of them had lived in countries that have suffered under the heavy hand of aggression and cruelty. Out of this meeting there came a better understanding of our own sins of racism and separation that have plagued Christians. This was indeed in answer to the Lord's Prayer that we might be one as He is One with the Father.

On another occasion in London, John wrote:

In my flight to London I was sick, and I hunkered down in my seat with a fever and a general feeling of weakness. But later when I faced my class of 33 students, something supernatural happened. I felt an uplift, a spiritual surge, and a challenge that brought forth reserves of strength that I did not know were there. My voice was clear and strong. As we studied and discussed "The Principles of Revival," not even the powerful gale winds that blew that night, or the week of cold and rain could dampen the spirit of this class. God is indeed good!

A recent trip to Russia showed that this country may be the greatest harvest field today. Our Korean Pentecostal Holiness brothers have moved in and have planted two churches in Moscow with a combined membership of 400 adults and 250 children. Churches have also been planted in Kazakstan, as well as in Uzbekistan with memberships of 330 adults and 500 children.

As the year was drawing to a close, John and Edna spent five days of wonderful hospitality in Hong Kong. These days with the Chinese Christians among whom they had lived and worked from 1978 to 1986 was full of warm gestures of a love that almost overwhelmed them. It was a privilege for John to preach in two of the five Sunday services at the great Wing Kwong church.

And then there was a lovely fellowship banquet held in their honor and in that of Miss Fannie Lowe, a dedicated nurse who had spent her life to enrich these people. It gave a golden touch to their stay among these wonderful people.

Costa Rica's 50th year Anniversary Celebration:

A highlight of the year was the Costa Rican 50th Anniversary Celebration, and it was a very special time of confirmation for the 23 years of John and Edna Parker's work there. General and conference officials, missionaries and representatives from different parts of the world were present as well as those who had served in Costa Rica as pastors, preachers, evangelists, teachers, and church planters. John and Edna Parker, and other missionaries who had served in Costa Rica over the years were honored and given special presentations by the nationals.

Here are excerpts from the September 1997 *Worldorama:*

Our hats are off to the nationals of Costa Rica for their recent celebration which marked the 50th

135

anniversary of the International Pentecostal Holiness Church in Costa Rica. Representatives from nine nations gathered in San José, the capital, to attend the <u>Vision America Congress.</u> Between 3,000 and 4,000 attended the sessions which were held in a rented facility in order to accommodate the large crowds...

Many ranked the Congress as one of the greatest events of this type they had ever attended. All of the planning was carried out by the nationals making it even more special. The Costa Ricans attribute the success of the event to the months of prayer and fasting which preceded the Congress. There were flags, banners, singing, and dancing! There was no business—just worship and praise to God. Coupled with the joyful celebration there were times during the morning, afternoon, and night sessions when people stayed prostrate before the Lord and tremendous utterances of prophecies came forth.

Elvio Canavesio, overseas ministry coordinator, said:

The Shekinah glory appeared to us for three days. Powerful utterances from God indicated that the Lord is pleased with us, and that He will use our church as a platform to reach the world with the gospel. It was a never-to-be-forgotten experience with God!

What a blessing that this very special event high-lighting what John and Edna Parker had begun at the beginning of their ministry should come at this pre-cise time when their missionary career was drawing to a close. They had started with just a few, but be-hold the harvest had become a multitude!

In the Parker's last newsletter of 1997 to their supporting churches, they made an announcement concerning their future with the World Missions De-partment. This statement, which came as a surprise to many, was at the very beginning of their corres-pondence.

This is the last newsletter you will receive from Edna and me as full status missionaries of the International Pentecostal Holiness Church. As of December 31, 1997 we officially retire. As we glance back over 52 years of ministry, we can only say, "God is faithful."

It was not easy for John and Edna to describe their feelings as they took this step, but they were at total peace with themselves, the church, and the Lord. A look at the past led them to declare that God had been their Guide during the many fruitful years of ministry. They had invested themselves in the lives of countless faithful men and women. These would continue to teach the Word, be instant in season and out of season, and they would strengthen and plant churches to extend the gospel of the Kingdom. And John and Edna would face the future with that same faith and trust. They would continue to be faithful to *Go and Tell* the wonderful story of God's love, His provision and His grace!

Chapter Nine
The Missionary's Message

When confronted with the possibility of reading the life story of a person, we often ask ourselves: What does this person really believe? What is important to him? What is his primary message? This Easter sermon by John Parker gives us the answers to these questions. His commission from the Lord was to go into the world and tell the message of salvation to others. That was his passion!

Go and Tell

The command, "Go and Tell" was given by Jesus through an angel on the morning of His resurrection. It is recorded in the Gospel according to Matthew 28:7:

And go quickly and tell His disciples that He is risen from the dead; and, indeed, He is going before you into Galilee; there you will see Him. Behold, I have told you.

John Parker

We also find the same instructions in Mark 16:7:

But go, tell his disciples--and Peter--that He is going before you into Galilee; there you will see Him, as He said to you.

This command, *Go and Tell*, includes both an activity and a reason for that activity. In Matthew 28:19-20, the command is reinforced:

Go therefore and make disciples of all nations, baptizing them in the name of the Father and of the Son and of the Holy Spirit, teaching them to observe all things that I have commanded you; and lo, I am with you always, even to the end of the age.

In Mark 16:15, this commission is repeated again.

And He said unto them, "Go into all the world and preach the gospel to every creature."

Thus we have not only the activity of going, but also the message that accompanies it. The followers of Jesus were to spread themselves abroad upon the earth and proclaim the message that God has raised Jesus, His Son, from the dead.

The resurrection of Jesus as a single event, however, has little value in itself. To have value and meaning, it must appear in conjunction with its divine antecedents, that is, the laying down of Jesus' life on the cross for the making of atonement, the satisfaction of God's judgment against sin, and the fulfilling of God's redemptive purpose for mankind.

It was the perfect work of Christ on the Cross that made possible His rising again from the dead. Jesus' resurrection was the glorious affirmation and the divine authentication that God was fully satisfied with the work of His Son. On the day of Pentecost, Peter declared that...

God raised Him up again putting an end to the agony of death, since it was impossible for Him to be held in its power (Acts 2:24, NAS).

Jesus had to rise again because of (1) the perfection of His life in holy obedience to the Father, because of (2) the surrender of Himself as a full-payment sacrifice for sin, and (3) the perfection of His victory over Satan and the kingdom of darkness.

The Scriptures are replete in their assertion that only on the Cross did Jesus suffer for our sins. The classic chapter in Isaiah 53 is a dark and awesome portrayal of what happened on that Cross—the grief, the sorrow, the striking, the smiting, the afflicting, the piercing, the crushing, as well as God's abandonment of His Son. Wave after wave of God's divine wrath swept over Him as He accepted, with no resistance, all the punishment and torture that man's sin and rebellion has accrued through all time.

Genesis 3:15 declares that in the midst of the agony, the Serpent's head would be crushed, as indeed it was. The disarming of "rulers and authorities," and "making a public display of them" was done on the Cross (Colossians 2:15). Beyond the Cross, there was no further conflict or suffering on the part of God's chosen Lamb. When Jesus cried, "It is finished," the struggle was over and the victory was assured. All the spiritual beings of the world of light as well as those of the world of darkness knew the issue was settled once and for all.

Most of all, Satan knew it was over. His crushed head left him in no disposition to celebrate high carnival with his stunned followers because the Son of God had died. On the contrary, Satan understood all too well the implications of that dying. In total defeat, he retreated deeper still into the shrouds of darkness that inevitably surround him.

On the other hand, Christ, the Triumphant Victor, commended His spirit into the loving hands of an adoring Father, and descended into Paradise where the spirits of the righteous dead were retained. For three days, all of this glory, triumph, and victory were hidden from the eyes of mortal man. Even the closest followers of Jesus went into mourning, losing temporarily their faith, but not their love for Him.

On the third day, God raised Jesus from the dead, an act that was stamped with marvelous majesty and overwhelming power. Paul described it in Ephesians 1:19 as being "...in accordance with the working of the strength of His might." G. Campbell Morgan wrote, "Simply to read this is to feel the irresistible throb of omnipotence."

In raising Jesus from the dead, God rejected every man-made system of salvation and every false culture of cynicism and indifference, as well as every political force of arrogance and assumed authority.

The Father has *"seated Him at His right hand in heavenly places, far above all rule and authority and power and dominion and every name that is named..."* (Ephesians 1:20, 21, NAS).

In the light of these verities, where are we to go and what are we to tell? For go we must and tell we must. Jesus made it clear in Acts 1:8 that we are to go to all people, even to the remotest parts of the earth. There will be no ocean too wide, no mountain too steep, no jungle too dense, no city too big, no desert too dry, no climate too cold or hot, and no circumstance too difficult or unpleasant. On the day of

Pentecost, God forged an army of intrepid soldiers, filled with the fire and power of the Holy Spirit, and set them in motion. They are still on the move.

What are we to tell? In Mark 1:15, it is the gospel. In Luke 24:47, it is that repentance and the forgiveness of sins, be preached to all nations. In Matthew 28:18, 19, it is the making of disciples of all nations. In Acts 4:10, it is the proclamation of the Name of Jesus who was crucified, but whom God raised from the dead. In Acts 16:31, it is to believe in the Lord Jesus and be saved. The crucified, resurrected, and ascended Christ is our message, the center of the center. It is He Who brings salvation, deliverance from the power of sin, and the bright hope of living forever in His glorious presence. May His joy and peace also be ours.

John Parker

Easter Message

Just as surely as Jesus arose from the grave, we shall also rise and be changed!

Behold I tell you a mystery: We shall not all sleep, but we shall all be changed—in a moment, in the twinkling of an eye, at the last trumpet. For the trumpet will sound, and the dead will be raised incorruptible, and we shall be changed.

Chapter Ten
The Missionary's Retirement

C an a pastor, preacher, teacher or missionary really ever retire? He may resign from his church
or change his field of work as a missionary or teacher, but can he really retire? Perhaps it depends on
who a person is working for. Is he employed to work
for a department or church, or is he there because he
has been called and commissioned by God? If he is
working under God's divine call, that call doesn't
change even if his area of ministry does. He will be
aware of that call as long as there is life!

Quite often it is ill health that takes a person out
of the field of service. In that case, the minister may
not be able to carry on his work. But there is a possibility that he/she may still have options to serve as
a minister of helps, an intercessor, a prayer warrior,
or an encourager via telephone, Face book or some
other electronic devise. Even though the area of
work or the job description may change, the call
doesn't. Those who are called of God find ways to
fulfill what has been placed in their hearts as long as

they are able to do so, even though it may only be on a one-on-one basis.

December 31, 1997 was the official date for John and Edna's retirement from the World Missions Department (now called World Missions Ministries). As this time in their lives rolled around, they decided to analyze what they had done in the past— a time of reflection on what they had seen during their years of service in the Department and to remember the wonderful opportunities of global ministry that World Missions Ministries had opened to them!

John and Edna had ministered in some 35-40 countries on innumerable means of travel from jet planes to oxcarts and even to dugout canoes. Their beds had ranged from luxury suites to dirt floors, and they had eaten all kinds of food that had been set before them. They had planted the seed of the gospel in many places, and they had seen them sprout and grow from tender shoots into sturdy plants. They had seen the works begin, mature, and reach out to extend the gospel into other nations of the world. In it all, they had been content and satisfied. God had been good to them.

John Parker had taught in advanced ministerial training programs in many parts of the world: in London at CICM, in Latin America in CURSUM, in Asia in AMTC, in Spain in the Mustard Seed Institute and in churches and conferences as they were needed. John's teaching had been shared with national church leaders in these training sessions. In fact John and Edna had always kept to the strategy that Jesus instituted and that was so ably put into action by His disciples. It was the strategy of the Apostle Paul in his world-wide ministry, and he stated it in his letter to his spiritual son, Timothy, with the following words:

And the things that you have heard from me among many witnesses, commit these to faithful men who will be able to teach others also (2 Timothy 2:2).

They were never unaware of the many people who had stood with them with their prayers and finances during their years of service. How could they ever adequately say "Thank you" to them? What loyalty they had exhibited! They had opened their arms, their homes, their churches, and their purses. John and Edna from the depths of their hearts could only say a big "Thank you!" And there were those missionary peers with whom they had worked, as well as the hard working directors, office staff in Oklahoma City and the compassionate women of Women's Ministries who had been "doers" in demonstrating their love to them.

147

They were being honored with cards and letters, phone calls and words of appreciation. They cherished them all. But it is always good to hold dear the words of appreciation that come from the director of the department under which you are working. It was good to hear from Rev. Donald Duncan, the director of World Missions Ministries.

M. Donald Duncan, Director
Missions Ministries
International Pentecostal Holiness Church

July 26, 1998

To John and Edna Parker:

You have faithfully served the Kingdom of God through the International Pentecostal Holiness Church…[and] this involved leaving family and home to go wherever the Lord would lead.

For twenty-three years you served in the beautiful country of Costa Rica helping to firmly establish the Pentecostal Holiness Church. Your strong leadership there prepared you to serve as a General Supervisor serving Asia, Europe and the Middle East. For the last four years you have served as a missionary on special assignment doing what you love to do—teaching. You have taught in the advanced ministerial training programs wherever needed around the world.

On behalf of World Missions Ministries we want to say thank you for your years of service. You have willingly gone wherever there was a need and filled that need with spiritual wisdom, grace, and dignity. Only our Heavenly Father has a complete record of the souls won, students trained for ministry, and churches built as a result of your love for a lost and dying world and your unselfish giving of yourselves and your talents.

Thank you, John and Edna Parker. We love you and pray that the years ahead of you will be as fulfilling and fruitful as those you have completed.

M. Donald Duncan

For John and Edna, of course, this was not the end of their ministry; it was just the completion of an assignment to teach God's Word to the world through the World Missions Department of the Pentecostal Holiness Church. But now what? They certainly weren't going to settle down into a rocking chair mode!

To begin with, John would still travel out of the country for three or four teaching missions a year as he was needed. There would also be invitations from different churches and special occasions. In addition, he had been designated as the Coordinator of Hispanic Ministries of the North Carolina Conference. In this position he would assist Director Chris Thompson in the development of the Ministries' work within the Conference.

John had previously been with Chris Thompson in the first Hispanic District meeting in the North Carolina Conference. It had been hosted in Rocky Mount, North Carolina at the Calvary Temple Church where the Hispanic Church, La Roca, had its services. It had been a great time in the Lord. Then on Monday night, John had taught a class on tithing and stewardship. His ministry had been a great blessing to the work at that time. There would be plenty to do!

And so it was as John wrote in the following newsletter:

We have not yet found a stopping place, either in our calling or in our labors. As a matter of fact, it seems that we have now come into that wide place of spiritual excitement that is characerized by a global harvest...The word "missionary" no longer means just white and western, for with them is that vast host of national workers God is raising up in virtually every nation on the earth. New seed is always the product of a harv-

est, and the harvest reaped from our efforts is becoming the seed of an even greater harvest for the future.

John received many invitations from different places as well as from his own conference. It was a surprise and also a special honor when the following announcement was made!

John and Edna Parker
"Mr. & Mrs. Missionary"
of the North Carolina Conference

What an honor to come from his home conference. John and Edna were appreciated and their work was honored and sponsored by these wonderful people. These were those who really knew them best!

Among different opportunities to minister, a special invitation came to John to give the main address at the Commencement Exercises of Holmes Bible College on May 24, 1998. It was a privilege to go back to the school where he had been a student and challenge those students who were graduating!

Dr. Richard Waters, President of Holmes Bible College expressed his appreciation in a letter he wrote on June 1, 1998.

Dear John,

I want to express my thanks to you for being our Commencement speaker at the Holmes Bible College Centennial Graduation. Your ministry was truly a blessing. All of us at Holmes, particularly our graduates, sincerely appreciated your excellent comments. Your very perceptive, meaningful and anointed remarks will long be remembered by all. Thank you so very much for being such a valuable part of the Holmes Bible College Commencement program...

In 2000, John spent a week in London at the Centre for International Christian Ministries (CICM) teaching a great group of students about World Religions and Cults. This would be the last time he would teach in this school since it was being closed to be replaced by a modular program which would focus on Europe. After 20 years of working with CICM, it was like saying good-bye to an old friend.

Retirement always means deciding where you are going to live, and John and Edna had decided to build a home in Fayetteville, North Carolina where they had some very good friends. They concluded later, however, that this was not exactly where they were supposed to be, so they sold the house and moved to Dunn—about 25 miles away from their previous location.

One of their very good friends in Fayetteville, who had been with the Parkers in different countries and ministries conducting teaching sessions, was John Hedgepeth, pastor of Northwood Temple. They enjoyed stopping in for times of chat and fellowship with Pastor John, and it was through this friendship that the Lord opened a new missionary opportunity for ministry.

John and Edna joined the Medical-Missions Team from Northwood Temple. Their destination: Nicaragua! They would be there largely as translators for the doctors and nurses, but John did the morning devotions for the team of about 50 people and preached in the Managua church on Sunday morning. During five full days of heavy work, they ministered medically and spiritually to about 1,600 patients. About 600 tooth extractions were made, and best of all some 200 people opened their hearts to receive the Lord as Savior.

It was in Nicaragua when the two Johns found themselves together as they looked out on the beauty of the landscape in front of them, that John Hedgepeth began to share something that was in his heart. For years Mrs. Ada Lee Thurmond, an anointed minister of the Gospel, had taught the Goodwill Adult

Bible Class at Northwood Temple. But she had gone on to be with the Lord, and Pastor John missed her. She had left a real vacancy at Northwood Temple, but now this pastor had something else to share with the other John:

> *John, you know you're just about 25 miles from Fayetteville, and that's just a few minutes on the interstate. Why don't you come over to Northwood Temple and teach that Adult Bible Class?*

It didn't take John Parker long to assimilate this invitation and to realize what it would mean to him to accept this invitation. It was a call to teach. This class, that numbered about 50 people, would keep him busy in the work he loved best. He would still prepare lessons, he would regularly teach, and he would have one-on-one contact with the same people week after week. So the invited John responded:

> *Well, John, if you twist my arm just a little, I just might accept that invitation!*

So it was decided, and John became the teacher of the Goodwill Adult Bible Class. It would take a very special place in John and Edna's ministry. John would prepare many of his own teaching materials since he was actually a Bible scholar in his own right. He would begin teaching as soon as he finished the commitments that he had already made.

A few days later John and Edna were on their way to Africa to keep one of those commitments! To visit Africa was the fulfilling of a lifelong dream. They spent two weeks in Kenya and enjoyed their All-African Retreat with the people there. Then there were four full days in Capetown, South Africa where John preached in two of the churches and also ministered to the student body at the Bible College. Another four days were spent in Johannesburg, and then there was a preaching assignment in Krugersdorp. From there it was on to Ghana where John spent five days with Stefan and Andrea Hall. He spoke on two different occasions: once to twenty-five ministers and then a preaching engagement on Sunday morning. John kept a very complete journal. What does his record tell us this time? On this trip they had been on ten different airplanes!

In April of 2003, the Parkers were in Costa Rica for the Third World Pentecostal Holiness Conference in San José. They were hearing great reports of what was taking place in the IPHC worldwide. It was exciting as well to read the statements of the vision and missionary goals for the coming years. Besides this, however, another highlight had been planned.

On Sunday morning bright and early they left San Jose for a bumpy but interesting two-hour ride for a time of celebration for the dedication of the Mount Zion church. It was being dedicated to God but in honor of the Parkers and their work as well. The funds for the project had come from Gospel Tabernacle of Dunn, North Carolina and from John's home church, Living Faith Fellowship.

Costa Rican Conference Superintendent José Salas said, *To talk about John and Edna Parker is to talk about the foundation and structure of the Costa Rican Church.*

Coordinator for Latin America, Dan Clowers, referred to the Parkers as people with an excellent spirit, like Daniel.

Edna Parker said, *We spent 23 years here, but now I am older, and I am so glad that I can see the fruit of our labors. I am very happy*

John Parker made a very typical statement as was his habit; he gave all the praise, honor and glory to God. He said…

I am especially happy that this is a service of honor and not a memorial! This service has very little to do with us and everything to do with God—so I give Him all the praise and honor, and my gratitude and appreciation to all who are present. I appreciate the pastor for his sacrifice and labor and vision. Good seed planted in good soil will produce its fruit.

Back in the States, John and Edna accompanied the Northwood Team on another medical-missions project. They had been with the Team to Nicaragua, but now it was Honduras. This trip was difficult, but also very fruitful. They had about 35 people in their team: doctors, dentists, nurses, and eye people.

They worked for three full days in the little town of Trojes, five hours across the mountains from the capital, Tegulcigalpa. The church building was over-crowded with a lot of different ministries going on, and crowd control was minimal. The frustration level rose to a fairly high point, but on Thursday night, the place was cleared out, and John was able to preach to a full house. It was great to see the receptivity of the people as they were blessed by the Lord.

Back in Tegulcigalpa John preached twice on Sunday to large congregations. Later he taught an 18-hour seminar on tithing to 15 pastors. The record shows that in the seven full days the doctors had ministered to 1,883 patients; the dentists did 357 cleanings, 183 sealants, and extracted 1,582 teeth while 581 people were fitted with glasses. Best of all, however, was that 204 people confessed Christ as Lord and Savior. God's anointing was rich and full there as John preached back and forth in both English and Spanish.

The Medical-Missions Team would continue to be busy. There was another trip to Nicaragua and then on to Guatemala. He would later go with a team from River of Life Church in Oklahoma City with Pastor Richard Goad. With that team they would minister: teach, preach, translate and work in Cuba.

John's work as the Adult Bible Class teacher during these "retirement" years was perhaps one of his greatest blessings—not only for the class, but also for him and Edna. Here he had a regular ministry where he was needed, and Edna, his faithful wife and motivator, was right there at his side. With God he had continued to move forward in ministry. His class did not hinder him from continuing to be a part of the Medical-Missions Team. This had become a vital part of their work during this time of…would you call this "retirement?"

John served as teacher of this Bible Class for 11 years—from 2001 to 2012. But change is always a part of the work of the Lord. David and his wife, Irvina, lived and worked in Oklahoma City, but they felt that their parents needed to be closer to them. David was director of the Extension Loan Fund of the IPHC, and Irvina was General Director of the Girls Ministry and had her office at the General IPHC Resource Center. David's mother would soon be 90 years old, and his father was not far behind her. They needed to be where he could keep an eye on them. They were fully capable of taking care of themselves as long as there were no emergencies. But David, as their only child was responsible for them and needed to watch over their well being. He felt this responsibility very keenly.

So John and Edna moved to Oklahoma City. They had to say "good bye" to so many: their friends and neighbors in Dunn, the ministers of the North Carolina Conference, and to the people of Northwood Temple – especially to the Goodwill Adult Bible Class! As to that…

John Hedgepeth said:

John Parker:

> *John did a great job as a teacher, and of course, he had Edna at his side as a motivator. They loved the class, and the class loved them. We will miss you, John and Edna. You are always welcome at Northwood Temple.*   *John*

Moving to Oklahoma City was not easy. David did the best he could and had an apartment all ready for them to move into. But there were no trees or outdoor living. Ms Edna walked through it and said, *I can't move John into this. He has to have more space!*

On a Sunday morning at River of Life Church where David was a faithful member, at the close of the service, people were invited to come forward, and Edna had a request:

We need a house. If you know of one, please let us know.

The next day, Harold Dalton, assistant director of World Missions Ministries, made contact with David:

I think I have a solution to the problem of John and Edna's housing! World Missions has a house designated for missionaries and we can let them rent it.

This duplex had been donated by Dr. Frank Tunstall in honor of his son who had died as the result of an accident. It was just what the Parkers needed, and they were deeply grateful. There was space in the front yard for the little flower garden Edna planted—designated "God's Garden." And there was a space in the back where they could also plant a few flowers as well as vegetables. It gave them something to do that they loved.

But things were so different for them. They were used to being surrounded by people who knew them and their ministries—people who often dropped in or those nearby that they could visit. In their new home, they felt isolated, and it was difficult to adjust.

But as has been said before, change is always a part of life. When Edna's 90th birthday rolled around, the River of Life Church, under the direction of their daughter-in-law Irvina, sponsored a grand celebration that will long be remembered. Friends from the local church, and conference and general officials were there to express their appreciation and to honor this tremendous lady who has been at the side of her husband, John Parker, for so many years.

In their new situation they depended on David and Irvina, and although they were very busy, it was great to have them when they could pop in. Then there were the grandchildren, and now the great grandchildren! How wonderful it was to be near them, play with them and see them grow!

There were also other friends from the past who helped fill in the gaps. There were Chris and Betty Thompson. Chris had been their Conference Superintendent in North Carolina but was now in the General Offices in Oklahoma City. Betty came and made it a point to take Edna to help buy groceries and at times to go shopping. And she would also take Edna to visit Jean Williams, the widow of Bishop J Foyd Williams who lives in a retirement home in Edmond, Oklahoma. Jean and Edna had been close friends at Emmanuel College years ago, and here in Oklahoma they could visit again. What a privilege!

Then there were missionary friends of the past like June and Elvio Canavesio who had moved back to Oklahoma City. What a blessing when they could come by now and then.

And there was Charlene West, a long-time friend, who had worked with them in Costa Rica. She had retired from the Hispanic church she had planted in Oklahoma City and seemed to feel the Parkers need for friends and fellowship. So she visits them one night a week to pray and read the Bible. Edna, of course, insists on her eating dinner with them every week on that night! She always prepares a delicious meal, and John sets the table and gets down that bowl that is just too high for Edna to reach! His comments on Scripture are always a blessing.

Sometimes others joined their little meetings like Luis and Liliana Avila who were also good friends and dropped in now and then to visit. They had directed the Hispanic work in North Carolina before becoming the General Director of IPHC Hispanic Ministries in Oklahoma City. They and people like Betty Thompson, June and Elvio Canavesio, Nuria and Carlos Bolaños, or other friends at times dropped in to bring something special, have a coffee, or share in a time of devotion.

Charlene West made a point of taking them with her to Hispanic meetings and also to General and Conference activities. Wherever John and Edna go, they are remembered and honored.

John Parker, Missionary Statesman, Teacher, Author and Bible Scholar: his life is one whose accomplishments cannot be counted out in numbers. He has prepared others who have prepared others, and they, in turn have prepared others.

But this story is not ended. John and Edna Parker have literally invested themselves in others who will continue to carry the torch of the Gospel. Those who have been taught will keep sowing the seed of the eternal Word they have been given. Lives will continue to be changed; the work of the Lord will grow, and the spiritual "children" of John and Edna Parker will continue to rise up and call them "Blessed!"

John Parker

*And the things that you have heard from me
among many witnesses, commit these to faithful
men who will be able to teach others also*
(2 Timothy 2:2).

This has been the life and ministry of John and
Edna Parker. The strategy of the Apostle Paul had
become their own during the many years of their
ministry. As a result, many who had been privileged
to sit under their teaching were giving to others what
they had received from the teachings of John Parker!

Chapter Eleven
What Others Have Said

This book is replete with what John and Edna Parker have done and said. But people who know them well have also had many wonderful things to say in appreciation of their work and ministry. It seems right to have these statements together here in this final chapter. Some have already been mentioned in other parts of the book. Our prayer is that as John and Edna read over these words, they may be a blessing and encouragement as they continue to walk with the Lord.

David Parker, son
Director Extension Loan Fund IPHC
March 25, 2014

John B Parker, my Dad

While those of you reading this excellent book about the life of my Father, John B. Parker, written in such eloquent style by Charlene West, know him as a friend, coworker, teacher or missionary, I am the only one that can write about John Parker as a father. I am an only child to John and Edna. God could not have given me a better set of parents here on earth. I was born on the mission field in Costa Rica on a Sunday morning and was in Sunday School the next Sunday. Yes, our lives revolved around church and mission work. They loved me, nurtured me, mentored me and set an example of what true Godly parents are to be here on earth.

My dad was always busy with the mission work but he always found time to be a Dad to me. He took me on many of the missions to the countryside, mountains and rain forest of Costa Rica. He taught me how to fish in the beautiful rivers and oceans that grace that lovely land. We spent a lot of time talking about nature, God, people and what was going on with the mission work. I will always cherish the times we had together.

In later life, his church work and my professional careers would keep us miles apart. But the times we were able to get together, holidays or vacations, he was always Dad and in later years a grandfather to my children. The stories are too numerous to be told in just one book and while I meet many people that talk about John Parker as a mentor, teacher, pastor, or mission director, I always just think of him as Dad. He set a great example of how a man can dedicate his life to the work of God and yet not ignore his own family.

Because of the model of a loving father that I experienced growing up, it was easy for me to accept the concept of a loving heavenly Father that I have never seen and to embrace His forgiveness and salvation. For being such a great father to me and my family, thank you Dad. We will always love you.

Your son, David

A.D. Beacham Jr., Presiding Bishop
IPHC General Superintendent
March 10, 2014

I will never forget my first missions experience in the summer of 1969 with John and Edna Parker and a team of IPHC young adults in Costa Rica. That summer I met a man, John Parker, that I came to greatly admire and respect. His humor, love for Jesus, and love for lost people impacted my life. I have often thought of a conversation he and I had late one afternoon on the porch of the building in Santa Ana. As a young college student called into the ministry, I was impatient for ministry and asked him whether I should continue in school or go directly into ministry. I will never forget his advice. He smiled, almost laughed, and with that touch of serious humor that he possessed, said, "Doug, you have more time than you think. Be sure to prepare all you can. The Lord will take care of the ministry part."

Through the years that sound guidance has guided many of my decisions. I have learned that the spiritual fruit of patience is related to preparation and trusting God's timing. I owe John Parker an eternal debt of gratitude for putting that wisdom in my life.

Years later I had the joy of serving with him while his missions' ministry expanded around the globe. We were together in England when his wisdom provided hope in a difficult situation. In the years I served as Executive Director of World Missions Ministries, I saw firsthand the global impact of John Parker and also Edna. They have left global footprints that continue to lead people to Calvary.

In this twilight season of life, the Lord is using John Parker in a different way… [and] the light of the Gospel of Jesus Christ still shines brightly in John Parker's countenance.

Rev. Chris Thompson
Gen. Director Evangelism USA
Oklahoma City, Oklahoma

February 3, 2014

John B. Parker – Friend/Mentor

It is a special honor to write a few words for John B. Parker – Statesman, Pastor, Teacher, Missionary, etc. I first met the Parkers in the mid-1970's after Betty and I had completed our studies at Holmes Bible College. We were in our first pastorate at Oak Ridge, and Bro. John came up to me at a conference meeting and introduced himself as a missionary. He was always interested in new pastors and young clergy.

During my second pastorate, the Parkers would visit our church on furlough. Our church supported them monthly and the church was near Sister Edna's hometown of Garland. John and I developed a close relationship during that time.

When Betty and I were leading the church plant in Cary, North Carolina, we also invited John and Edna to the church, and they were well received. They visited our home and fell in love with our three sons. John was always supportive and encouraging, and he freely shared from his vast experiences. Never was there a dull moment when we were together.

Allow me to fast forward a number of years to when I served as the North Carolina Conference Evangelism and World Missions Director. We were endeavoring to reach the Spanish-speaking people of North Carolina. Rev. Charlene West, IPHC National Director of Hispanic Ministries, had given several workshops across the Conference, and we were off and running. During the first couple of years we were somewhat successful with several churches planted but were met with several major challenges.

At that time John Parker was semi-retired from World Missions and had moved home to Dunn, North Carolina. He quickly became my Hispanic Coordinator and personal advisor. For several years we prayed, talked, preached and traveled thousands of miles together. We met with Anglo Pastors and Leaders and many Latino Pastors and Leaders. John Parker taught me how to understand the many Hispanic cultures and helped me develop a love and deep appreciation for the Hispanic people. This was easy for him as his teaching flowed from his heart.

The number of Spanish speaking churches increased to near seventy, and Bro. Luis Avila was hired as a full-time Coordinator and Supervisor. John had known him as a boy in Costa Rica, and at this point John became our official conference advisor. His advice was valuable and significant.

I can hear him speaking now when he was going to interpret for me: "Speak in complete sentences; flow with the anointing but slowly; stay in one place and remember, in translation I will correct your bad grammar and any bad theology." (I assume he did).

He was a delight to work with, because he was a man of integrity. I know his stories - preaching, the mission field, hunting, fishing. I have also done his income taxes for nearly twenty-five years. He is a man of God, I will always be indebted to him.

Thank you, Lord, for bringing John and Edna Parker into my life!

Chris Thompson

Leon Stewart
General Superintendent IPHC
July 17, 1986

When I think of your ministry, I feel like the Apostle Paul must have felt when he wrote *"I thank my God always concerning you for the grace of God which was given to you by Christ Jesus..."* Thank you for responding to the call of God in your life. Thank you for being willing to do something of eternal value in the world for Jesus' sake and for being a part of the world-wide outreach of the PH Church. We are glad that you are a part of us, and we're proud of you!

Donald Duncan
Director World Missions Ministries
IPHC – July 26, 1998

John and Edna Parker: On behalf of World Missions Ministries we want to say thank you for your years of service. You have willingly gone wherever there was a need, and you filled that need with spiritual wisdom, grace, and dignity. Only our Heavenly Father has a complete record of the souls won, students trained for ministry, and churches built as a result of your love for the lost and your unselfish giving of yourselves and your talents. We love you.

Hugh Morgan, pastor
Chaplain Statesman
University President
Hugh's News

John and Edna,

God has great plans for you, and I know He will continue to fulfill His divine purposes in your lives and the extensive ministries He is giving to you. God has signally used you in a number of phases of ministry, and you have done an excellent job in each of them. You have brought excellence into every mission God has commissioned you to do. And I, for one, will never forget your marvelous spirit, your patience, your knowledge of history, of the world, of cultures, languages, and peoples.

Ronald Q. Moore
President: Southwestern College
  of Christian Ministries

November 9, 1995

It is a joy to have the privilege to share with you that the Southwestern College of Christian Ministries Board has voted to bestow upon you the Honorary Doctor of Divinity Degree in honor of the life and ministry that you have exemplified. We love you and pray for your continuing ministry!

James D. Leggett
General Superintendent IPHC
February 27, 2008

I deeply appreciate your attending the annual conference of the Methodist Pentecostal Church in Concepcion, Chile to interpret for me. You did a great job... Faye and I very much enjoyed your fellowship. Through the years I have had great respect for your ministry in World Missions. I often refer to you as a missionary statesman, and I believe God has blessed you to be a leader in World Missions. You and Edna have been a tremendous blessing to so many. May the Lord's richest blessings be yours.

Philip M. Steyne
Columbia Biblical Seminary
December 20, 1991

As student papers came in, it was evident about what happened in the Mis 625 class. Several expressed appreciation to those of you who made such significant contributions to the class sessions…I add my appreciation to that of others for your specific contribution, free participation, and the balance you brought to the sessions. You have endeared yourself to us. …I pray that [God] will bring you an even greater world-wide ministry in the future.

John Hedgepeth, pastor
Northwood Temple
Fayetteville, N.C.

John Parker:

It is always nice to be among God's people, but it is particularly nice to be around you, because you have such a spirit of love and fellowship… John and Edna, I am amazed at the tremendous leadership that you have given our Missions Department. I believe that the Pacific ministries are the fastest growing, and we are thrilled to be a part of it. We know that it just doesn't fall in place. Somebody has to take the leadership. Your leadership stands out…Thanks for being you.

Missionary Statesman

Carolyn Foster
Missionary in Hong Kong

John and Edna Parker: It was my privilege to serve
with you for a number of years in Hong Kong. My
fondest memory is when you would invite all the
missionaries to your home to celebrate Thanksgiving
and Christmas. Being far from home, we all appreciated being together during that special time. John,
you would cook the turkey, and Edna prepared all
the trimmings. You served our church well in many
parts of the world, but I am so glad you were a part
of our family in Hong Kong. Your love for us as fellow missionaries was always apparent in your sincere desire to help us. Thanks and God bless you!

Dan and Brenda Clowers
Continental Directors
Latin America and Caribbean

John Parker is without a doubt one of the most
revered missionaries to ever work in Latin America.
He spoke perfect Spanish, but above that he taught
the Word from his great wealth of knowledge. Everywhere he traveled in our region the people honored
him. In Costa Rica, where we lived for 12 years,
they named the conference campgrounds after him.
He influenced thousands with his dignity and friendly approach. The book he wrote on Basic Doctrines

175

(*Doctrinas Basicas*) is still used as a textbook in many venues of continued education and will be used for years to come.

After Bro. John and Ms. Edna retired, they continued to visit us in Latin America and the Caribbean, teaching and ministering, and many times working long hours translating in the medical clinics. This was a great inspiration to us that showed us that ministry isn't just for the pulpit. We were blessed to have had the privilege of learning from Bro. John and working alongside him many times.

Richard Goad, pastor
River of Life IPHC Church
Oklahoma City, Oklahoma

In 2006, I led a group from the church I pastor, River of Life IPHC in Oklahoma City, on a special missions project we were undertaking to build a church in Guaninao, Cuba. To my delight, David Parker, one of our members, told me his father would love to be a part of our effort. It was a great joy to see our ministry efforts to Cuba suddenly gifted with the participation of a minister of such stature. John Parker was Missions in my mind. He had impacted Central America, Asia, and Europe in his lifetime of service in God's Kingdom.

It seems that one place he had always wanted to visit but never had was Cuba. With the cooperation of Bishop Beatrice Lopez of Cuba, we were able to offer a pastors' retreat at the Cuban IPHC Conference Center. John Parker, one of the greatest missionaries the IPHC has ever produced, was the primary speaker. It was humbling but extremely gratifying to observe the impact that his insightful wisdom in practical ministry issues coupled with his knowledge of scripture had with the ministers in that conference. I will forever be grateful to the Holy Spirit for orchestrating this amazing opportunity.

James and Barbara Dickinson
Missionaries in Costa Rica
North Carolina

We arrived in Costa Rica in December 1969. John and Edna Parker and their son David opened up their home for us until we found our own home. They helped us to learn to live in a foreign culture and to survive the culture shock.

John and Edna taught us what missionary work was all about, not just teaching and preaching which is important but things like evangelizing in areas difficult to reach, building thatch roof churches, outhouses for pastors, building bunk beds for the new

Bible School dormitories, things that are never taught in Bible School.

John was a true evangelist; he loved his work and the people loved him. John and Edna Parker influenced our lives in ways unnumbered.

Terri Dickinson West
Pharmacist – North Carolina

. John Parker was the missionary most respected, dignified in presence and eloquent of speech. He had a heart for God and a love and passion for the Hispanic people. I only know that to me, he was my Uncle John and that's the way I'll ever love him.

Terri

Bishop Dr. Frank Tunstall
Superintendent IPHC
Heartland Conference
Oklahoma City, OK

John and Edna Parker:

John and Edna Parker have given their lives and their entire ministry in missionary service. They are numbered among only a handful of IPHC missionaries to serve with distinction on three continents (South America, Asia, and Europe) in the first century of World Missions Ministries.

John and Edna went to Costa Rica as a young missionary couple and served in Costa Rica for 23 years. Their next assignment was Hong Kong, and later they became supervisors of IPHC missions in Asia. Their third overseas assignment was in Europe and John later became the supervisor of IPHC missions in Europe and the Middle East.

In 2006 the Heartland Conference of Oklahoma donated a newly remodeled missions house to World Missions Ministries. That duplex now serves as the retirement home of the Parkers. I honor John and Edna Parker highly, and look forward with genuine excitement to reading their biography.

Charlene West, Missionary
Pastor, Church Planter
Oklahoma City, Oklahoma

John and Edna:

I met you and your son, David, in 1969 when I chaperoned a Youth in Action Team to Costa Rica, and in 1970 I joined the Costa Rican team as a missionary with my children. You gave us a big welcome, but you also allowed me to minister in the gifts God had given me.

You were compassionate. I hadn't been a widow very long, and during my first year there, my Father went to be with the Lord. Thanks for caring.

Later we taught on the team for ministerial training courses in different parts of Latin America, and your work was always highly esteemed. You, Edna and David were like family. Now that you and Edna are senior citizens here in Oklahoma City along with me, I am glad I can still visit you. It is a special blessing to me to share God's Word and pray with you concerning our needs. God bless you as you continue to serve.

Kathy West Petty
IPHC Missionary
Granada, Spain

John and Edna Parker:

You possess the gift of "celebrating life." Your influence has been a vital thread woven through the story of my life for over 45 years beginning in Costa Rica as one of the "missionary kids," and then at Southwestern College as a young student. This continued later in Venezuela and Spain in service on the mission field. Thank you for all you have been and done for me and my family!

Kathy

Time Line

Costa Rica: 23 years
December 31, 1951 – 1974

Southwestern College: 4 years
1974 - 1978

Hong Kong/ Asian Ministries: 8 years
1978 – 1986

Pentecostal Bible Institute: Chile
2 years, 1986—1988

Europe and the Middle East: 5 years
1988 – 1993

Roving Missionary Professor: 4 years
1994—1997

Retired from World Missions Department 1997

Coordinator of North Carolina Conference Hispanic Ministries

Goodwill Bible Class, 2001-2012 (11 years)
Fayetteville, North Carolina.

Retired as Sunday School Teacher from N.C.
Moved to Oklahoma City, Oklahoma 2012

A final note from the authors:

This book was written from the newsletters, letters, and bulletins that John Parker received or wrote during the many years of his ministry. We were glad we had so much to be able to write this story with confidence. Some planned projects may never have taken place, but there is a world of evidence to prove that many of them did!

Thanks to you for being a part of this book.

Charlene H. West
Edna Parker

Books by Charlene West

English:
Close Out of the Ages
Life is a Great Adventure
Don't Miss the Rapture
John Parker, Missionary Statesman
(with Edna Parker)

Spanish:
Haciendo Discípulos por medio de la
Escuela Dominical
La Primera Resurrección
¿Qué haría si perdiera el Rapto?

Books by Edna Parker
Just Me
John Parker, Missionary Statesman
(with Charlene West)